Numerology and Tarot

Unlocking the Power of Numbers and Tarot Spreads along with Discovering Symbolism, Intuition, Numerological Divination, Astrology, and Ayurveda

Contents

Part 1: Numerology

Reveal the Secret Power of Numbers and Discover How Numerological Divination is Connected to Astrology, Tarot, and Ayurveda

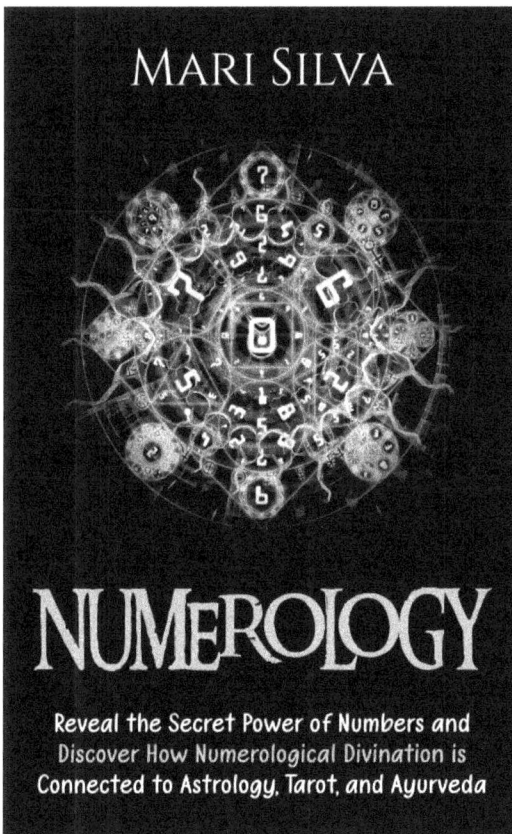

MARI SILVA

NUMEROLOGY

Reveal the Secret Power of Numbers and Discover How Numerological Divination is Connected to Astrology, Tarot, and Ayurveda

Introduction

Do you want to attract more positivity into your life? Do you want to improve any specific aspects of your personal or professional life? Are you curious to get a sneak peek at what life has in store for you? If yes, the answers to these questions lie in numerology.

According to numerology, everything in life can be reduced to a numerical value. All that happens in life and all your interactions with the world can be recorded in numerical terms. You may have discovered certain numbers resonate with you. You might consider some to be lucky or even attach a sentimental value to them. For instance, your loved ones' birthdate or even your birth date can hold significance. Certain numbers may remind you of something special such as your anniversary, the day you got your first job or any other special occasion. From the prices of goods to anything you come across in life, everything has a specific number.

Consciously or subconsciously, the entire world is governed by numbers in one way or another. Numerology is the science of understanding the connection between numbers and your life. By learning about numerology, you can learn about your inner motivations and discover your true self. You can also learn about what motivates you and others. Think about all the benefits you can gain by doing this - from making better decisions to reconnecting with your inner self, numerology plays an important role in all aspects of your life. It allows you to analyze different personalities, discover your inner affinities, and make the most of the opportunities that present themselves in your life. This is not a new concept but has been around for thousands of years. Time and again, science has also proved the benefits of numerology.

The uncertainties of the future can make life a little overwhelming. In such instances, getting a sneak peek of all that destiny has in store for you can be helpful. Well, if you are eager to do this, it is time to learn about numerology. The good news is everything you need to know is provided in this book. This book will act as your guide every step of the way.

In this book, you will learn about the origins of numerology and how it works with your personal birth date, and the numerology of your name. You will learn about the theoretical aspects of numerology and how you can calculate your life path number, destiny number and how they are related. From daily cycles and patterns to the nine-year cycle, you will understand what's in store for you. You will learn the role numerology plays in your love life and relationships with others. Once you are well versed in all these basic topics, this book teaches you to create a chart using all this information. It also introduces you to the relationship between numerology and Ayurveda, tarot and astrology.

So, are you eager to get started on this journey of self-discovery by using numerology? Do you want to uncover any hidden talents or opportunities that will help you to fulfill your destiny? Let's get started!

Chapter 1: Origins of Numerology

Numbers not only hold a numerical value but spiritual value too. Numerology helps demystify the relationship between numbers and their personal energies. Numerology is also considered as the study of the numerical values associated with different letters of the alphabet. If you are familiar with the imaginary world of Harry Potter, you may know that arithmancy was Hermione Granger's favorite subject. Even though many details aren't included about arithmancy in the series, it can be inferred that it involves the magical properties of numbers. Hermione often uses several complex charts and divination to predict the future using numbers. Numerology is the real-life equivalent of arithmancy.

History of Numerology

Numerologists believe numbers influence everything that happens in the world. Everything depends on their mystical properties. All their perceived mystical properties result from the energy vibration inherent to numbers. Vibration is the term commonly used by new-age practitioners to describe the inherent power in certain items such as gemstones, colors, essential oils and crystals. It is not just crystals and gemstones that have energy, but even numbers do.

In numerology, it is believed that every number has a unique vibration that gives it special properties. These properties can be used to understand an individual's behavior or even predict compatibility in relationships. Numerological analysis can determine an individual's lucky number or days. Recurring numbers can be used to obtain clues about how the world works and the significance of different individuals or events in one's life. Numerologists strongly believe there is no such thing as an accident. Everything that happens ultimately boils down to numbers.

The ideas of numerology are not new concepts. The earliest records of numerology date to ancient Egypt, Babylon, China, Japan, Rome and Greece. Pythagoras is credited with the creation of the system of numerology. He was an ancient Greek philosopher born in 569 BC. Historians know only a little about this famous philosopher because most of his original work did not survive the test of time. Also, the historical mentions of Pythagoras were written by individuals who came hundreds of years after his time. This is one reason why some historians believe the discoveries often attributed to Pythagoras were created by his followers later.

The followers of Pythagoras are known as Pythagoreans. Pythagoras studied music, philosophy and mathematics comprehensively. One of the most important discoveries associated with the Pythagorean School of thinking is the Pythagorean Theorem. According to this theorem, in any right-angled triangle, the square of the hypotenuse's length is always equal to the sum of the other two sides' squares. Does this ring any bells? The Pythagorean Theorem is summed as $a2 + b2 = c2$. This is one of the basic mathematical theorems taught in school. Pythagoreans are also believed to be the ones who discovered the first irrational number or the Pythagoras' constant - the square root of two.

Besides these discoveries, Pythagoras and Pythagoreans also believed that numbers have inherent mystical properties. This belief stems from the discovery that adding up a series of odd numbers, starting with 1, results in the square of the concerned number. These discoveries further strengthened the belief of Pythagoreans that "all is numbers." It essentially means that everything in the world can be measured and described numerically and in proportions. The "all is numbers" belief also suggests the world is purely made of numbers, and everything can be reduced to a numerical value. Well, this idea is logical, and it has a significant influence on math and science.

While studying mathematical concepts, Pythagoreans sorted all numbers into different categories. For instance, numbers such as 1, 4 and 9 are squares because the corresponding number of pebbles or dots can be arranged in the shape of a perfect square. Likewise, 1, 3, 6 and 10 are triangular because the corresponding pebbles or dots can be arranged into shapes of regular triangles. Another observation is that numbers such as 2, 6 and 12 are oblong because, when arranged, the corresponding number of pebbles will form rectangles.

Pythagoreans not only described numbers in mathematical and geometrical terms but also according to their non-numerical traits. These traits have little to do with science or math and are more to do with intuition and mysticism. For instance, even numbers were considered feminine, while odd numbers were thought of as masculine. The number one is associated with creativity since adding multiples of one often creates another number. Similarly, number two is feminine and represents duality, while three is all about masculinity. A combination of two and three represents marriage because it is the midpoint of numbers one through nine. It also represents justice. Ten is believed to be a sacred number because it is the sum of the first four digits. These beliefs helped to create ten fundamental opposites such as odd and even, right and left, masculine and feminine, straighten crooked, light and darkness, square and oblong, good and evil, one and many and odd and even.

The interest in mathematical mysticism increased after Pythagoras's death. It quickly gained prominence in the form of neo-Pythagoreans during the first century A.D., but the interest in the non-mathematical theories proposed by Pythagoras soon faded away. During the late 1800s, several books about the concept of number vibration, music and colors were published by Mrs. L Dow Balliett. Several other writers might have published their works before her, but it was her books that brought to light the relationship between Pythagorean principles and other concepts used in modern numerology.

A general philosophy followed by all numerologists is that every number has a specific vibration. It's not just numbered, but people, places, food and even objects tend to have their own vibrations. For instance, certain places, people and foods make us happy. Why does this happen? It happens due to the constant flow and exchange of energy in the universe. To live a happy, harmonious and productive life, we all must ensure our environment vibrates in sync with our energies. It is not just numerology that concentrates on this vibration of energies. Some new-age practices believe this vibration results from the movement of subatomic particles.

Certain schools of numerology believe this vibration results from the music of spheres. It essentially backs the Pythagorean belief that celestial bodies make a specific sound while orbiting the Earth, but this belief was disproved by science because the Earth and other planets orbit around the sun, and it isn't the other way around. This is where modern numerology makes up for the flaws present in the Pythagorean concept of numerology. Modern numerologists use numbers to make sense of the universe instead of relying on intangible concepts.

How Numerology Works

In life, there are no such things as accidents. It might seem as if your birth date and name are seemingly random, but they have deeper meanings and reasons. Numerology is a treasure chest filled with helpful information. By understanding the hidden meanings of numbers, you'll have the key to unlock the treasure chest.

Numbers hold a special significance in certain religions too. For instance, in Christianity, the number 888 is believed to be the representation of Jesus, while 666 is considered the number of the beast. Let us not forget about the holy trinity or that Hanukkah lasts for eight nights. According to Chinese tradition, number four is believed to bring bad luck. The system of numerology is used in modern times to discover the hidden meanings of the world.

Most use numerology like astrology. We use it to predict the future and as a tool for self-discovery. A common reason people turn to numerology is that it helps them understand their life's purpose. Life can be confusing and overwhelming. By calculating your life path and destiny number, you can learn more about your characteristics, unique personality traits and even weaknesses. These numbers can remind yourself of your true purpose in life, finding the ideal profession and creating healthier relationships. You will learn more about calculating these numbers in the later chapters.

Numerology can also help you make better decisions and choices in life. Every decision you make changes the course of your life. By choosing a path that matches your numerology chart, it becomes easier to create a life that's happy, fulfilling and rewarding.

Numerological readings can establish and maintain healthier and happier relationships. Knowing more about yourself and the personality traits of others in your life makes it easier to maintain relationships. When you understand all this, it becomes simple to form and maintain positive and lasting ties. A solid understanding of your basic traits makes it easier to manage any expectations in a relationship.

Your life path number helps you understand your strengths, weaknesses, and other personality traits. It also determines any favorable or unfavorable periods. It comes in handy while preparing and planning for important events in your life, such as changing your career or embarking on new relationships. Similarly, your destiny number can reveal what you will do in life. The destiny number combines the numerical values associated with the alphabet of your full name. A combination of one's destiny and life path number can be used to make important decisions.

Since numerology gives you a better understanding of yourself and life in general, it becomes easier to deal with any obstacles that happen during your life. Likewise, it makes you more aware of all the potential opportunities.

Chapter 2: Your Birth Date in Numbers

If you are working hard to improve your life, it means you are moving a step closer to your goals every day, but the lack of important information about your life path number may be holding you back. By using numerology, you can get a better understanding of yourself. If you are new to the world of numerology, you have likely heard about different strengths associated with life path numbers. Good and bad are two sides of the same coin. This balance is the rule of nature, so every life path number not only has certain strengths but weaknesses too.

It becomes easier to overcome challenges caused by the shadow side of your life path number by understanding them through numerology. The life path number is based on your date of birth, and can determine your life's purpose while giving you better clarity about the different opportunities available. In this section, you will learn how to calculate your life path number and different exercises you can follow to overcome any weaknesses associated with that.

Calculating Your Life Path Number

To harness the power of numerology, it is important to determine your life path number. No worries – it's incredibly simple to calculate. It is essentially the sum of your full birth date. It is a representation of who you are at the moment of your birth. It also helps determine your personality traits, drawbacks, and different talents. To get started with calculating your life path number, you only need your birth date. It includes the date, month and year in which you were born. The next step is to convert all the numbers into single digits. For instance, if you were born on 17th February, you need to add 1 and 7, which gives you 8. There is one important consideration while doing this. All numbers need to be converted into single digits except the numbers 11 and 22. For instance, if you were born on 11th February, leave the number as it is. Remember this rule because it applies to birthdays that fall on the 22nd of a month or the total of digits, which end up in 11 or 22. In numerology, 11 and 22 are considered *Master Numbers*.

Here is a simple example to get a better understanding of how to calculate your life path number. Let us assume that you were born on 22nd November 1994.

November 11th (month) - 11

22nd (date) - 4 (2 + 2)

1994 (year) - 23 (1 + 9 + 9 + 4)

Now, add all these numbers and you end up with 38. So, the life path number in this case will be 11 (3+8).

For instance, if someone was born on the 10th March 1980, the date and month will be 1 and 3, respectively. By adding all the individual digits in the birth year, you will arrive at 9 (1 + 9 + 8 + 0). There are three single-digit numbers associated with the individual's date, month and year of birth, which are 1, 3 and 9, respectively. Now, it is time to add all these numbers until you are left with a single-digit number. The sum of all these numbers is 13. So, the life path number is 4 (1 + 3).

Do you realize how simple it is to calculate your life path number? Now you know how to do this, so the next step is to understand each number's strengths and weaknesses.

Life Path Number 1

Individuals with life path number 1 are creative and dedicated. It essentially means you have an inherent tendency to stick to your goals without getting distracted by other things. The most effective techniques that can attract more positivity into your life are visualization and creating a dream board. On the downside, those with this number care too much about others' needs, desires and opinions, so you probably might be trying to achieve goals that don't mean anything to you. Your inherent desire to please others takes away the courage required to live the life you want.

Suitable Exercises

The simplest way to overcome the weaknesses associated with this number is to concentrate on activities that help you get in touch with your personal values. For instance, take some time and list five things that mean the most to you. These things need to add value to your life, even if it means you gain no praise from others or are subjected to external criticism. Once you have this list, ask yourself what different goals can be set to live by your personal values. Anything that is not in sync with your values adds no real meaning to your life. The activities you need to concentrate on are the ones that hold to your values. Use your creativity and dedication to become more confident, independent and autonomous to live a life you desire without worrying about others.

Life Path Number 2

Individuals with life path number two are genuine, sensitive and extremely honest. Tuning in to their heart's desires and emotions is quite easy for them. On the downside, they can feel dejected and hopeless when faced with criticism and difficulties in life. Instead of looking for solutions to the problems or obstacles, you end up wallowing in negativity about all the possible things that can go wrong in any situation. This fear can prevent you from taking the desired action to achieve your goals.

Suitable Exercises

To overcome the challenges associated with life path number two, concentrate on developing and maintaining a positive mindset. To let go of your negativity, ask yourself where the negative thoughts stem from. What does your inner voice say, and where do you think it comes from? Perhaps it is a teacher, a friend, a family member, or even a mentor. Make a note of the different self-defeating beliefs and assumptions that play in a loop within your mind. Try to reframe all negative thoughts into positive ones. For instance, instead of thinking, "I cannot do this," or "I am not good enough," reframe it as "I cannot do it right now," or "I am capable of achieving my goals." Question your negative thoughts instead of accepting them as the absolute truth. The shadow side of this number brings lethargy, so try to elevate your energy levels and adopt a positive mindset.

Life Path Number 3

Individuals with life path number three are blessed with a socially magnetic personality. Whether it is networking, personal relationships, or anything else that involves others, you have a significant advantage over others. These individuals are optimistic and filled with inherent positivity that help them achieve their goals. On the flip side, they can be uncertain and have a tough time with commitment. Finding one thing to concentrate on and achieving it can become challenging for those with life path number three, so you must try to devote all your energy toward one goal instead of several goals at once.

Suitable Exercises

Since life path number three comes with a shadow side of difficulty with commitment and focus, mindfulness is a great way to ensure that you stay in the moment. It allows you to concentrate and focus on only one thing at a time. The simplest way to do this is by concentrating on your breathing. Spend around 10-15 minutes daily focusing on your breathing and nothing else. Don't worry about anything and allow your thoughts to drift. By staying in the moment, it becomes easier to focus on one task instead of unnecessarily squandering your energy through multitasking.

Life Path Number 4

Individuals with life path number four are practical and have a strong will. These know what they want and come up with a practical plan to achieve their goals. On the downside, since they are so focused on what they want, their perspective is rigid. This rigidity prevents them from seeing any opportunities that come their way. They may also struggle with manifesting wealth into their lives.

Suitable Exercises

The good news is managing and manifesting wealth into your life is not a difficult task. A simple way is to use the Law of Attraction to determine what you need the finances for, the desired quantity and concentrating on Earth. From visualizing the financial success you desire to daily affirmations, there are several techniques you can use. By thinking and maintaining a positive attitude and beliefs about money to expel negative beliefs, it becomes easier to obtain the financial success you want.

Life Path Number 5

Individuals born with a life path number five are open-minded, creative and flexible with out-of-the-box thinking and solutions. Instead of worrying about the future or past, you are good at staying in the moment and aware of current experiences. The shadow side of this can make them self-indulgent, concentrate only on transient pleasures of life, and not see the bigger picture. It is important to not only maintain a positive attitude about yourself, but it is equally important to project this positivity toward others in your life.

Suitable Exercises

Since this life path number can make you self-focused, it will do you good to think about others. Instead of worrying about your own goals and dreams, try to do your bit for others. A random act of kindness with no expectation is a great way to bring balance to your life, so make it a point to do one good deed daily. It can be something as simple as grabbing a coffee for a coworker or talking to your friend when they need you. Once you focus on the bigger picture and not just your own life, you will automatically feel better. Stay in the present, but if everything you do is chasing transient pleasures, you will attain nothing significant or meaningful. Think and plan for the future without letting go of your inherent mindfulness.

Life Path Number 6

Life path number six is associated with compassion and generosity. These are individuals who spread goodness wherever they go. They are blessed with a nurturing nature and high levels of energy. A combination of these factors makes it easier to maintain the right kind of positive attitude in life. The shadow side of number six makes it difficult to balance giving and receiving. If all you ever do is give and then give more, you will have nothing left for yourself. It can also make it increasingly difficult to concentrate on the things you love and cherish.

Suitable Exercises

Since these individuals are nurturers and givers, it is important to concentrate on self-care. What good can you be to others if you cannot help yourself? Remember, even safety instructions in flights suggest you need to put on your own oxygen mask before helping others. Let go of the little voice in your head that tells you it is selfish to look after yourself. Prioritizing self-care is not selfish and is a sign of self-love and compassion. Ensure that your deeds add value to your life before helping others.

A simple way to do this is by listing different things you appreciate about yourself. Don't let these traits be determined by what you can do for others. For instance, some traits you can include are creativity, dynamic and helping nature, or even good listening skills. This list will act as a reminder of your self-worth. The next step is to concentrate on doing the things you love and enjoy. This is the only way you can add value to your life. By concentrating on yourself, you can increase your self-esteem, self-respect and establish healthy personal boundaries.

Life Path Number 7

Individuals with life path number seven are peace loving and have serene energy radiating from within. They are reflective, too, and adept at maintaining bonds with others without letting it define their lives. Maintaining and nourishing healthy and well-balanced relationships is your secret power. On the flip side, they may struggle to appreciate all the good in their life.

Suitable Exercises

To let go of this number's shadow side, it takes a conscious effort to connect with your intuition and spirituality instead of solely depending on the analytical aspect of your mind. Maintaining a gratitude journal and meditating are two simple activities to bring about a sense of positivity to your life and mind. Every day makes a note of at least 3-5 things you are grateful for. This is an effective way to let go of any negativity you might harbor while focusing on the silver lining in all the obstacles you face, but doing this will take conscious time, energy and effort. With practice, you will get better at doing this.

Life Path Number 8

Individuals with life path number eight are incredibly determined, focused, and thoughtful. They are also practical and confident, which makes them great at organizing. The shadow side of this life path number means the practicality you desire leaves little or no room for dreaming. It can also make it difficult to connect with your emotional side because your analytical mind rules your life. These individuals are also susceptible to concentrating too much on materialistic possessions that leaves no room for emotional value, so cultivating and maintaining lasting love isn't always easy for them.

Suitable Exercises

The simplest way to overcome the weaknesses associated with this life path number is by connecting with your emotions. Don't ignore or repress them, but allow yourself to feel whatever you feel. There is no judgment here, so stop ignoring your needs. Once you accept your emotions and determine their source, any discomfort associated with them goes away. It is time to go back to the basics and concentrate on every emotion. What do you feel about different emotions? What caused these emotions? How were you conditioned to deal with your emotions? By answering these questions, you get a better idea of what your emotions mean and why you feel the way you do. It allows you to connect with your true feelings to better understand your wants, needs and desires in life. How can you achieve your goals if you are uncertain of what you want or why?

Life Path Number 9

Individuals with life path number 9 are quite honorable and blessed with a sense of fairness. These traits make others automatically respect them. They are also incredibly charismatic and have magnetic personalities. By learning to harness this magnetism, they can attract all the good they desire in life. The only problem is the 9's shadow side can prevent them from doing this. These individuals can develop an unhealthy obsession with achieving success in their lives or attaining financial freedom. The negative thoughts they have about the things they desire effectively prevent them from attaining their goals.

Suitable Exercises

The first step toward overcoming the weaknesses associated with this number is to acknowledge your beliefs. If there are any negative beliefs about the things you truly desire in life, it's time to reform the beliefs that prevent you from succeeding. A simple activity you can follow is to note a specific goal you have in life. After this, surround this word with as many positive beliefs and associations as you can. For instance, if finances are important to you, you can write good associations such as "It will let me travel as much as I want," "It allows me the freedom to experiment," or "It means I don't have to worry about my future." By doing this, you are essentially manifesting your thoughts into reality. You are trying to attract the positively required to attain your goals without faltering along the way.

Life Path Number 11

The life path number 11 is one of the master numbers and numerology. Individuals with this number are blessed with spiritual awareness. Others might perceive them to be someone who knows more than they do. They also have a special gift of insight. They have plenty to offer to the world around and always dream big. On the shadow side, they are prone to severe mood swings and swing between extremes in life. They also struggle to feel grateful for all the good they have in life.

Suitable Exercises

The most effective and straightforward means to overcome the weaknesses of the shadow side of this life path number is by concentrating on emotional balance. Learn to shut down the inner critic in your head to manifest your true desires. The simplest way to do this is through meditation. Through meditation, you can calm your mind, stay in the moment and pursue your dreams and desires. Instead of allowing your emotions to guide the way, learn to manage your emotions.

Life Path Number 22

The other Master Number is 22. It is believed to be the most powerful life path number of all. These individuals are blessed with a powerhouse of positive energy, which can make the world a better place. Even though it is a powerful number, it comes with its own set of challenges. It is highly unlikely they are negative, but they can become overbearing and self-censored. These traits increase the risk of self-sabotage and prevent you from reading the life you desire.

Suitable Exercises

Become mindful of how you communicate with yourself and others in general. Learn to strike a balance between being insincere and tactless. By expressing your authentic self, it becomes easier to achieve your goals and dreams. For instance, list all the things you struggle to say. After this, it's time to look for how you can say them without hurting yourself or others. Personal development exercises can help you overcome the challenges associated with this number and free up more space for yourself and all that you want in life.

Chapter 3: The Numerology of Your Name

There is no such thing as an accident in this life. Everything that has happened, is happening, and will happen is all the manifestation of destiny's work. What do you use every day but never pay for? Time to put on your thinking hats. Well, do you know the answer to this riddle? If you don't, the answer is your name. We use our names daily but never pay for them. Often people think, "What's in a name?" Well, your name is not an accident. Even if it seems like something you were bestowed with at birth, it shapes the course of your destiny. Every letter of your name actively shapes your reality.

Remember, in the previous chapters; it was mentioned that every number has a specific vibration? Since every letter of the alphabet corresponds with a specific number, your name has a unique vibration; it is the true reflection of your life's purpose. The vibrations associated with it helps shape your unique personality and perception of life. As with your birthdate, even your name is of utmost importance in numerology.

In the previous chapter, you were introduced to the concept of life path numbers and the different traits associated with them. Now, it is time to add another tool to your numerology toolbox- the Destiny number. Sometimes, certain qualities associated with your life path number correspond perfectly with your personality, but there will be certain parts that don't make complete sense. If that's the case, it means you are missing some vital information. Your destiny or expression number provides this vital information. The destiny number or expression number is an important aspect of numerology and it complements the life path number.

The life path number offers a one-dimensional projection of who you are. The name suggests it helps identify the primary purpose of your life. Once you combine this number with the destiny number, it helps you understand how you will achieve your purpose projected by the life path number. When you combine these two ingredients, it helps create a complete profile of who you are and how to achieve your destiny.

For instance, if your life path number is one, then you are a go-getter. This number is associated with originality, creativity, leadership, initiation, competition, action and immense confidence. By placing your destiny number on top of the life path number, you understand how you can achieve the purpose set out by life path number one. The destiny number essentially sets the bar you need to live up to. It is similar to any expectations you might have of yourself or other people's expectations of you. It essentially offers insight into how an individual will express his purpose set out by the life path number.

Let's go ahead with the previous example of life path number one. If the destiny number is two, you might experience certain internal conflicts because number one is about independence, leadership, achievement and individuality. But destiny number two is all about harmony, love, balance and paying attention to group dynamics. Do you see how the basic traits associated with these numbers can create conflict? But it does not mean these numbers are an impossible combination. Instead, every combination comes with its own set of brilliant potential and strengths.

The only thing you need to do is understand how you can maximize and increase your strength associated with each number while reducing any weaknesses so they work in harmony. When you know your life's purpose, it is important to understand how you can achieve that purpose.

The destiny number helps reveal more about your life's purpose. It offers insight into how you need to live your life and all the different things you need to do to achieve your purpose.

Since it offers this insight, it becomes easier to note all the different opportunities that might present themselves in your life. It's not just opportunities, but it also helps identify any potential obstacles or hurdles you need to overcome to manifest your life's purpose. It helps understand what your destiny is and how to achieve and express your true purpose. Another benefit of understanding the destiny numbers is that they enable you to make the most of all the life experiences. Showing you the bigger picture, and the things you need to do to get there, makes you more mindful.

Calculating Destiny Number

Do you want to learn how to calculate your destiny number? If yes, grab a sheet of paper and write down your full name that you were given at birth. Don't forget to write all of your middle names – if you have more than one. One rule to remember is you can skip the Jr., Second, Third or any other suffixes.

According to numerology, every letter of the alphabet corresponds with a specific number. This number is determined by the positioning of the number in the alphabet. For instance, the letter Q is the 17th letter, and the number it corresponds with is 8

(1+7). If this sounds too cumbersome, create a chart using the positioning of each number. Here are the different letters and their corresponding numbers.

A, J, S = 1

B, K, T = 2

C, L, U = 3

D, M, V = 4

E, N, W = 5

F, O, X = 6

G, P, Y = 7

H, Q, Z = 8

I, R = 9

Here is a simple example to give you a better understanding of how to calculate your expression or destiny number by using all the letters of your full name (birth name). Let us calculate the destiny number of John Winston Lennon.

The first step is to break down the full name into the different numbers the letters are associated with.

JOHN WINSTON LENNON

So, the name John corresponds with the numbers 1, 6, 8 and 5, respectively. By adding these single-digit numbers, you get 20. Whenever required, add the numbers to ensure you obtain a single-digit number. The number associated with John is 2 (2+0). Repeat this step for calculating the numbers associated with Winston and Lennon in this example. The calculations are:

John = 2 (1 + 6 + 8 + 5)

Winston = 33 (5 + 9 + 5 + 1 + 2 + 6 + 5)

Lennon = 11 (3 + 5 +5 + 5 + 6 + 5)

Note: While calculating the destiny numbers, you shouldn't reduce the master numbers (11, 22 and 33) to single digits but should leave them as they are.

Now that you have the individual numbers associated with the individual's first, middle and last name, it is time to calculate the expression number. The expression number is the summation of all these numbers. John Winston Lennon's expression number is 46 (2 + 33 + 11). This can be further reduced to 10, which gives the expression number 1 (1 + 0).

Understanding Destiny Numbers

In this section, let's look at the strengths and challenges associated with it. In life, we can all use a little extra advantage. You can get this advantage by understanding yourself, your purpose – and how to manifest this purpose. To do this, you need to have an in-depth knowledge of your strengths, weaknesses and any potential challenges you need to overcome. So, let's learn more about all this.

Destiny Number 1

Creativity, entrepreneurship, and leadership traits are associated with this number. Destiny number 1s are destined for greatness and authority in whichever field they choose. Achieving independence, trusting your creativity and turning your ideas into reality are things you strive for in life. The confidence to transform your dreams into reality increases as you mature and grow.

On the downside you might not have the required confidence to follow your ideas, especially when stuck dealing with authorities. It can be difficult to sit by and watch as others get all the opportunities you feel you deserve. Learn to harness your inner leadership skills while honing your listening skills to shatter glass ceilings like you dream of doing.

Destiny Number 2

Individuals with destiny number 2 are blessed with a strong sense of intuition, are natural healers and value relationships deeply. They strive to create a life filled with beauty, peace and harmony. Whether it is your personal or professional life, partnerships hold a special appeal. On the flip side, you might give too much of yourself to others so you have nothing left. Instead of the world around, concentrate on the world within, and focus on your dreams and aspirations. Learn to use your natural empathy by tuning into your intuition.

Destiny Number 3

Everyone is drawn to their charismatic and magnetic personality and a smile that lights up the room. These individuals are inherently optimistic, and their joyous and creative personality acts as a people magnet. Their strengths include self-expression and the ability to express their thoughts effectively and efficiently. Your sensitivity that can be your strength can quickly become a weakness too. This sensitivity increases self-doubt and prompts self-criticism. The only way to move ahead is by letting go of your inner critic, who induces self-doubt.

Destiny Number 4

Individuals with this destiny number are honest, hardworking, blessed with leadership qualities and dependable. You love passionately, and your love knows no bounds. There isn't anything you wouldn't do for your loved ones, especially family. Working toward success and leading others comes naturally to you due to your entrepreneurial abilities. All the good that's within you wish to share with others. Unfortunately, you stand the risk of burning yourself out while trying to help others. Remember, even when you intend to help others, offering unnecessary advice and telling others what to do can make you seem bossy and domineering. Try to use your natural traits to help attain your goals while working with others as a team.

Destiny Number 5

Individuals with destiny number 5 value their freedom more than anything else. They are naturally talented, creative and have multiple areas of interest. A charming personality, curious nature, a need to explore and wonderful storytelling abilities make them attractive to others. Since you are drawn toward multiple things, settling with one option might not appeal to you. This can make your life seem more complicated than it needs to be. Learning to focus on a single task without getting distracted is one skill you need to learn. Remember, being with someone doesn't mean less freedom for you. All that matters is how you deal with relationships in life. By setting and implementing personal boundaries, holding onto your love for freedom is easy.

Destiny Number 6

This destiny number makes you feel a strong sense of responsibility toward others, especially your loved ones. You detest the thought of letting anyone down. You desire success coupled with harmony and peace. These individuals have a strong inclination toward a perfectionist attitude, and everything needs to be the absolute best. This stands true especially when you lend others a helping hand. The only problem with this destiny number is you tend to do things for others at your own expense. Let go of your perfectionist attitude to get anywhere in life. No one is good at everything, and we all need help occasionally.

Destiny Number 7

Individuals with this destiny number have a keen sense of seeking truth in any situation. You are insightful, and the way your mind works is similar to an X-ray. Your brilliant sense of intuition, coupled with an understanding of the universe's mystic ways, ensures you are always on the right track. These individuals require a career that allows them to work independently to make the most of their sharp mind and intuition. On the downside, it might not always be easy to trust yourself. The only way to get over this is by learning to trust your intuition. If your internal voice says something is amiss about a situation, it's probably right.

Destiny Number 8

This destiny number belongs to all the individuals capable of seeing the bigger picture. While most of us are overwhelmed by the little things in life, they step back and understand the role they play. They love to be in charge of things, usually form the upper rung of management, and are good at managing resources. Status, money and power are a few things you long to be comfortable with. Once you understand your destiny as a leader, managing the resources available at your disposal becomes easier.

If you feel unworthy of your achievements, it's not just the wins you need to prepare yourself for, but the losses too. Even when it feels like you have no control over your life, you do. By improving your self-worth, you can automatically feel better about yourself and your purpose in life. It also brings you a step closer to your destiny while eliminating self-sabotaging beliefs.

Destiny Number 9

These individuals are natural counselors, teachers and blessed with a deep sense of intuition. Their deep intuition, coupled with wisdom and spiritual insight, draws others to them. You always stand up for the underdog and use your spiritual gift to share success with others. On the downside, you probably give too much to others or don't receive enough for all the effort you make. You have an inherent desire to be of service to others, and it can leave you exhausted and tired, so an important lesson these individuals need to learn is that life is not just about giving but receiving too.

Destiny Number 11

This destiny number is considered spiritual. You have the power required to manifest your dreams into reality. As a natural-born leader and spiritual teacher, you can use your words to inspire others. Your magnetic persona automatically draws people toward you. Once you let your intuition guide the way, you will become unstoppable.

It becomes easy to doubt yourself because of your fine-tuned vision. 11 is a master number and so it comes with great potential and challenges. Don't doubt your vision for the future; listen to your gut and let it guide the way. You can use meditation to calm your mind and strengthen your intuition.

Destiny Number 22

This is a master number that brings with it an enormous potential to manifest your goals into reality. You have an inherent drive to leave behind a legacy that will help generations to come and not just the existing one. Incredible intuition and practical nature are two important traits that help attain the success you desire, not just in the physical realm but also in the spiritual one. You want to lay down the foundations for not just your family but wish to do something good for the world in general. This destiny number is a master builder and a natural teacher.

There is a lot of potential within you, but this potential also comes with its own set of challenges. When you want to help so many people, it's easy to feel as if you are responsible for them all. This can quickly become overwhelming and consume you. It is okay to want to help others, but it is equally okay to let others help too. To be successful, concentrate on your self-discipline and patience. Also, don't forget to look after your physical and emotional wellbeing.

Destiny Number 33

As with destiny numbers 11 and 22, this one is different from all the other single-digit numbers. Individuals with this number showcase quality similar to the numbers 3 and 6. You are creative, expressive and talented and wish to transform the world. Selflessness, generosity, energy and artistic inclination are defining traits of these individuals. They have a maternal vibration and are natural caregivers. You are also perceptive, kind and intuitive, but your desire to help others can quickly drain you of your energy. You might also face certain challenges with self-expression. Since number 6 is deeply associated with service, you might believe others need your attention more than you do. This distracts you from understanding and believing in yourself.

Core Numbers

Let's look at certain core numbers everyone needs to be aware of. You cannot make the most of numerology's various benefits until you learn how to understand the different numbers.

The first number you need to understand is the life path number. Perhaps this is one of the most important numbers you will ever calculate and use in numerology. It is derived from your date of birth. This reveals some vital information about the ideal direction for you and life and all the different lessons you must learn. It essentially provides a very broad outline of all the different opportunities and challenges that await you. It also gives better insight into your personality traits that will help make this journey easier and fruitful. To calculate the life part number, you need to add the different digits that make up your birth date.

The expression number is the second number you learn to calculate after the life part number. It is derived from all the different numbers present in the letters of your full name. Your full name is the name you were given during birth. It includes no suffixes. The expression number is used to get a better understanding of your talents and abilities that have been present since your birth. It is also known as the destiny number or the potential number.

The heart's desire number is calculated by adding the different vowels present in your full name. Once again, the name we are referring to is the name you were given at birth. It helps get a better insight into your souls' deepest desires, likes and dislikes and everything else you keep private.

The personality number is calculated by adding all the consonants in your full birth name. All your surface traits are revealed by this number. It offers information about how you like to dress, your sense of style and how you usually interact with others.

Another number calculated using your birth name is the hereditary number. It is the sum of all letters present in your last name. The last name is also known as the family name or surname. It offers insight into your passive personality traits. It essentially refers to the traits shared by family members and is a part of your heritage. Understanding this number makes it easier to ensure your energy vibrates in sync with that of your family members.

The growth number is the sum of all the letters of your first name. The growth number often acts as a modifier to the life path number. It helps identify a pattern that promotes your growth and development in life. You can use this information to develop the required skills required to ensure you are on track, revealed by your life path number.

Chapter 4: Your Lifepath Plus Destiny Number

We all have a maturity number in numerology. The energy associated with this number manifests itself when we enter our 40s. It is a little fascinating and surprising that everything in numerology has a precise calculation and the maturity number is the only exception. The energy, manifestation, and the influence of this appear gradually. You can see it by the ages of 35- 50. It's quite similar to driving down on a highway and seeing all the billboards. While you navigate life following your life path number, the maturity number gives you a better understanding of your final destination. This helps you understand where you are heading – whether or not you fully realize it.

Since this usually manifests itself as a midlife message, it might feel like you hit a transformation or changing point. In some ways, this number is a precise indication of your true self. After you have completed the first phase of life, the years associated with all thoughts of "been there and done that," the second part begins. The maturity number guides this portion. It's a common belief in the community of numerologists that the maturity number isn't in full force until an individual reaches 50 years of age.

A defining characteristic of the maturity number is that you are suddenly filled with additional energy. This energy can make you feel as if you don't have sufficient time or the patience required to waste on things that aren't propelling you toward your goal. This is one reason why individuals experience life-changing moments once they enter the 30s. You don't have to worry about it because it is your maturity number at play.

It is quite easy to calculate your maturity number. It is the summation of your life path number and destiny or expression number. Here is a quick recap of how your life path and destiny numbers are calculated. Add all the numbers in your birthdate to obtain the life path number. The destiny or expression number is the sum of all the numbers corresponding with the letters in your full birth name. Don't hesitate to refer to the detailed steps discussed in the previous chapter for these calculations. Once you have both of these, merely add them to obtain your maturity number.

The maturity number is also known as the realization of a real number. For instance, if your life path number is 5 and your destiny number is 9, your maturity number is 5 (5 + 9 = 14, 1 + 4 = 5). Now, it is important you understand more about each of the maturity numbers.

Maturity Number 1

This number is associated with independence, so individuals with this maturity number are often reevaluating their idea of independence and know what it means to stand on their feet. It encourages you to take the initiative, step into the role of a leader, and take on calculated risks to achieve your goals and passions. The one area where this maturity number will challenge you, includes situations when the need for independence takes precedence over everything else.

Sometimes, your sense of independence or dependence is highlighted. It also influences how you connect and relate to those around you. Are you wondering what all this might look like for you in life? Well, you must reevaluate your self-centered behaviors. Don't ignore your inherent desire to break free of any situations where you are dependent on others. This maturity number brings with it a dramatic change in your financial situations due to life transitions such as illness, divorce, or anything else along these lines.

Maturity Number 2

This maturity number essentially suggests you are reevaluating your emotional sensitivity so it benefits you and others. It means life is calling you to make the most of your diplomacy. It encourages you to contribute toward creating and maintaining healthy relationships, and to get involved with others and work in groups. The primary challenge associated with this number is it sheds light on all issues associated with your sensitivity. Sometimes, your sense of self in a relationship is called into question; you need to modulate your oversensitivity and concentrate on maintaining healthy relationships.

Now is the time for self-introspection to understand if you have been insensitive to others. Self-centered behaviors that might hurt others are undesirable. Try to look beyond yourself and become a part of groups to contribute to the greater good. Understand that yourself worth stems from within, and you don't need external approval. So, stop being a doormat for others.

Maturity Number 3

This number indicates you are trying to understand what it means to be expressive, filled with joy and creativity. It encourages you to embrace your creativity, spend more time with others and learn to express yourself. The most common obstacles faced by those with this maturity number are associated with creativity that suddenly takes center stage. Situations could challenge your ability to enjoy life, communicate effectively, interact with others and your sense of enthusiasm.

The best way to break free of all these things is by expressing yourself through artistic means. The sky's the limit, and there are various forms of self-expression you can use, such as writing, dancing, singing and other art forms. Understand that life comes with its own set of emotional ups and downs, and you need only to live through them. Once you live your life in alignment with your creative self-expression, luck, comfort and abundance will enter your life.

Maturity Number 4

Understanding what it means to work with limitations is what this maturity number is about. It essentially means this number is guiding you to work effectively and efficiently to reach your goals, create systems and processes which will help you again the goals, and leave a legacy that adds value to this world. Any issue associated with limitation and restriction is commonly associated with this maturity number. Sometimes, you need to change your attitude and become more optimistic while tackling the situation one step at a time. Instead of getting overwhelmed by any adversities, try to understand the difference between being rigid and being dogmatic. Managing and delegating are two important aspects of life but micromanaging merely drains your energy.

So, don't be surprised if you come across events where you need to determine the difference between a responsible and irresponsible course of action. Similarly, it's time to evaluate any self-defeating thoughts or behaviors based on inherent feelings of restriction. Examine the different ways you can shift, change and mold your life to attain professional and personal goals.

Maturity Number 5

Maturity number 5 means you are evaluating what it means to work with independence and freedom. Now is the moment to think about how you can constructively use freedom, add flexibility to your life, cope with uncertainties and embrace the concept of progressive change. The most common challenges faced by this number include the ones caused due to inherent conflicts about discipline and the use of freedom. It is okay to crave freedom and embrace uncertainties of life, but self-discipline is important to attain your goals and ideals.

Don't be surprised if a dramatic change comes up in your life, and it makes you evaluate your sense of freedom. From your child leaving home to divorce or a death in the family, such events can make you question the idea of freedom. It also gives you a chance to think about how you can get what you want from life. If you cannot control your excessive indulgence, especially when it comes to alcohol, food, sex, or drugs, it will become problematic and result in unproductive activities.

Maturity Number 6

It helps you understand what it means to work toward helping others and your family. You have a sense of duty to be of service to others. This number calls upon this inherent sense. You tend to live your life through compassion and affection. The most common challenges associated with this maturity number are associated with modulating responsibility. Sometimes, you might engage in meddling behaviors, display self-righteousness and test the strength of your intimate relationships. These issues can also crop up while you are trying to provide compassionate service to others.

This maturity number is associated with freedom, especially financial freedom that comes via an inheritance or marriage that lets you live the comfortable life you desire. It is a great time to concentrate on your personal life, especially home and family matters. Allow your artistic creativity to concentrate on being of service to others.

Maturity Number 7

Living your life using introspection and spiritual contemplation is what this maturity number is about. You want to understand your true self acts as a homing beacon, showing you the way. The most common challenge you need to deal with is associated with seeking the truth. Sometimes, you need to isolate yourself from others to understand what you desire. You can turn toward research and writing to find spiritual enlightenment and inner peace you so desire.

This maturity number manifestation is characterized by a personal crisis that makes you reevaluate your core beliefs. Your need for solitude and self-introspection make you value the concept of personal space.

Maturity Number 8

This maturity number suggests that you are trying to understand what it means to enjoy the rewards you get through accomplishments. It encourages you to make the most of your talents, coupled with your managerial and organizing abilities to fulfill your achievements. If you use your authority wisely, you can achieve the success and recognition you desire. This number often accompanies a shift in life that brings forth issues associated with achievements in the physical world. Sometimes, you need to step up into the role of a leader and direct others. It's not just about accepting financial abundance and wealth but working for the benefit of society too. It's not always about personal games in life.

If you want to make the most of the guidance offered by this maturity number, look for opportunities that use your managerial, leadership and organizing abilities. This maturity number may bring with it a significant change in your chosen vocation or career. You might also find a new motivation to concentrate more on your professional life to build a career or focus on work instead of concentrating solely on personal relationships, so it's important to maintain the perfect balance between personal and professional lives to make the most of the guidance offered by this number.

Maturity Number 9

The maturity number 9 is all about learning to be of service to others without expecting anything in return. It encourages you to work toward giving and contributing to the general good of society expecting no personal rewards. It helps let go of yourself and think beyond your own needs and desires. It teaches you to let go of particular outcomes while concentrating on tasks. A primary issue you need to watch out for which comes with this number is it can be slightly challenging to balance others' needs with your own. It is okay to be of selfless service, but it is not okay to ignore yourself and your life. Contact your inner philanthropist and teacher without burning yourself out. Understand that self-care is as important as being of service to others.

Master Maturity Number 11

All master numbers bring with them a sense of spiritual purpose. This understanding   is true for maturity number 11 too. This maturity number essentially suggests you are on a conscious path toward understanding what it means to harness your emotional sensitivity to help yourself and others. You are also pushed to use your diplomacy and get involved with group dynamics while keeping yourself open to relationships. You are essentially an introverted extrovert and are working toward fame and leadership. The common issues associated with this maturity number can challenge your creativity, sensitivity and the ability to overcome obstacles. The challenges you face are associated with the intensity with which you live life.

Master Maturity Number 22

This master maturity number prompts you to reevaluate what it means to manifest your dreams into reality on a grand scale. It calls out to your inner leader and manager to come to the forefront. Guided by spiritual principles and armed with practical know-how, you can achieve your goals and help others to lead better lives. One area you need to pay attention to will be communication. It's okay to be opinionated but coming across as a know-it-all is undesirable. Temper your bluntness and don't be too rigid in your approach to life. Try to think outside your box, strike a balance between self-care and hard work, to overcome any limitations that may result from your actions.

Chapter 5: Daily Cycles and Patterns

Understanding Daily Cycles

A great thing about numerology is you can use numbers to identify patterns and make daily forecasts about what you can expect every day. By now, you will have realized how important they are. From your birthday to your full name, everything can be simplified to single digits. These numerical equivalents help us obtain some insight into what life has in store. Everything comes in cycles. Everywhere you look, there are numbers, cycles and patterns. All you need is the right information to make the most cues you see in your life.

Unless it is a master number, every significant number of your life can be reduced to a single digit. You don't need your birth year to calculate the daily number. The important numbers you need to do this calculation are your birth month, birth day, current day, current month and the current year. For instance, if you want to know your daily number for December 25, 2020, and your birthday is 30th July, this is how you calculate your daily number.

Since your birth month is 7, the number is 7. Now add the day of your birth, and you end up with 3. Since December is the 12th month of the year, the number is reduced to 3. The desired daily number you are checking for is the 25th of December, which is 7. The desired daily number year in question is 2020, which gives you 4. Now, it's time to add all the single-digit numbers. In this case, it will be 7 + 3 + 3 + 7 + 4, which is 24. So, your desired daily number for 25th December 2020 is 6. Now, let's look at what each of the numbers signifies on any given day.

The interpretations for different numbers are based on the vibrations given by each of them in numerology. It essentially shows the subtle energy or attraction that will flow into your life during a day due to a specific number.

Personal Day Number 1

This number brings with it an energy good for planning new projects or starting new ventures. Is all about self-determination and self-sufficiency. If you are thinking about joining the gym, eating healthy or doing any new activity, today is the day to get started. The subtle energy that resonates with number one helps you get started and do things on your own without worrying about approval.

Personal Day Number 2

By now, you will have realized there is a pattern that each number follows. Their primary traits always stay the same. The energy associated with number 2 resonates with working in groups. It is a great day to work with a team. It allows you to be considerate of other people's feelings and give you the energy to defuse situations with diplomacy and tact. On this day, concentrate on your relationships, and it will be worth your while.

Personal Day Number 3

Number 3 brings with it a lot of creative energy, which will help your self-expression. An ideal outlet for all your creative expression is through social interaction. This energy is filled with optimism that makes life seem better and gives you the strength to tackle any problems that happen in your life. If you need to meet others, attend important meetings, or just interact, number 3 will give you the required energy.

Personal Day Number 4

The energy which resonates with number 4 is organization. Its methodical energy helps you understand that the best way to complete tasks at hand is by doing them the way they were completed before. This consideration helps you think about securing a stable foundation for your future.

Personal Day Number 5

Personal freedom is what number 5 is associated with. Today's energy gives you the inner desire to express yourself and test your personal liberties. Take this opportunity to engage in different activities that seem to inspire you. It becomes easier to look at life from multiple perspectives without getting bogged down by your single perspective.

Personal Day Number 6

Your life's primary areas that resonate with the energy given out by number 6 are your family and home. This gives you a chance to nurture and support all your loved ones. Not just your loved ones, but this energy can also do good for society in general. It makes you compassionate, giving and nurturing. If there is a specific social cause or an idea that appeals to you, work on it today.

Personal Day Number 7

We often ponder about different questions that concern our existence. What is of purpose on this earth? What are our goals? What do we desire? And so on. Number seven's energy encourages self-introspection. It helps you understand that the answers you are seeking will not come from an external source but are present within. Whether it is science or spirituality, this is a great day to accumulate knowledge and wisdom. Trust your intuition to guide the way and work on solving the mysteries within.

Personal Day Number 8

Finance is one aspect of life; most of us struggle with it. Dealing with any form of financial stress can induce great levels of anxiety. Whether it is planning for a secure future, thinking about your savings or investment, or clearing debt, today's the day for this. Accumulating, managing and maintaining materialistic possessions and finances requires patience and an ability to think about the future. These two things become easier when the energy of number 8 is on your side.

Personal Day Number 9

The energy that resonates with personal day number 9 makes you think about society's welfare and the world in general. It will inspire and motivate you to think about how you can contribute to others and not just yourself. Use this day to be of service to others. Think about how you fit into the bigger picture.

Personal Day Master Number 11

The personal energy that resonates with master number 11 is steeped in spirituality. Intuition, peace and harmony are the main ingredients radiated by this number. Today is a great day to focus on anything associated with spirituality. Whether it is your relationships or avenues that help you step into the role of a teacher, indulge in them. The energy of 11 includes all the good vibrations associated with personal day number 2.

Personal Day Master Number 22

The subtle energy vibrations of number 22 give you the strength to manifest your ideas or thoughts into reality for spiritual and social benefit. You will feel organized, practical and filled with a renewed sense of self-confidence, making it easier to work with others. Work with others and use the cooperative energy of 22 to achieve a shared goal. This number also includes the positive energy associated with personal day number 4.

By extending the different energies associated with the personal day numbers, you can gain insight into what lies in store for you every day. Stop wondering, "What will happen tomorrow?" Or "Why do things happen the way they do?" And calculate your personal day numbers. With the power of numerology, it becomes easier to obtain an overview of the potential each day offers.

Understanding and Interpreting the Numerical Patterns

Since numerology is all about numbers, seeing patterns in them is common. If you stumble upon repeated patterns, it is believed to be a sign from the cosmos or the universe. Seeing certain number sequences repeatedly is a message that your energy vibrations are synchronized with the universe, and you are receiving guidance or support from your spirit guides. Since every number has a unique vibration, you can determine the message your spirit guide of the universe is trying to communicate with you based on the sequences you see. Common sequences are 111, 222 and so on. Seeing three numbers in a row such as 333, 444, 111, and so on is a powerful sign from the universe. So, heed this intuitive message by deciphering the meaning of each number. Here is a brief overview of what each number means in numerology and the significance of patterns.

- Number 1 is associated with independence, originality and leadership traits. The appearance of this usually signifies the start of something new.

- Number 2 is about the association, cooperation and sensitivity. This number's appearance is a sign you need to be more cooperative and work with others to achieve your goals.

- Number 3 is associated with self-expression, creativity and a desire for spirituality. The universe is sending you a message about different opportunities available to you based on your creativity.

- Career, stability and professional relationships are denoted by number 4. Seeing this repeatedly can be a warning about a situation associated with your professional life.

- Number 5 brings with it a sense of higher consciousness, adventure and excitement. If you repeatedly see this, it is a sign that good things are in store for you.

- Number 6 is associated with your personal life and family in general. Repeatedly seeing patterns with 6 means you need to concentrate more on your familial ties and responsibilities.

• Number 7 expresses a desire for alignment with your spiritual side. It essentially conveys the message that some opportunities help synchronize your inner self with the cosmos.

• Abundance and prosperity are associated with number 8. If you constantly see patterns with this, it is a sign the universe is sending you guidance to attract abundance and material wealth into your life.

• Number 9 brings with it a deep sense of accomplishment that feeds your soul. If you repeatedly see these patterns, it is a message you need to start concentrating on your life's real purpose.

• Number 11 is a master number that conveys the message; it is time to listen to your intuition and let it guide the way. It can also be a sign you are about to meet someone whose energy vibrations will help increase yours.

• Number 22 is the master builder which is a sign from the universe you have what it takes to manifest your dreams, thoughts and ideas into reality.

The guidance from your spirit guides or the universe often presents itself as a sequence of numbers. Use the information given until now to understand the message the cosmos is trying to communicate. Patterns can come in sets of twos, threes or even fours. For instance, you might see 11, 111 or 1111. What is the difference among these three? The number of ones that appear correspond with the strength and power of the message sent by the universe. If you repeatedly see 111, it means your intuition is at its peak, and it is an opportunity to share your gifts or creativity with others, perhaps through teaching or accepting a leadership role. It can also be a sign it is time to start something new.

222 carries forth the energy of unconditional love and acceptance. If you repeatedly see this pattern, it means now is the time to understand, accept and act on your heart's desires and express yourself clearly. It is also a gentle reminder for you to open yourself up to others and work on forgiveness.

The energy vibrations of 333 are associated with emotion and creation. Seeing this pattern means your body and soul are working in tandem to create and manifest your desires. It is the perfect time to open yourself up to the world and express yourself effectively to tap into your potential.

The energy vibrations of 444 are associated with dreams and hopes. Believe that you can achieve anything and are on the right path toward attaining your goals when you repeatedly see this number pattern. Lay down the foundations for your greatest dreams and believe in yourself that you can see things through. It also suggests financial abundance will soon enter your life.

Change is an important part of life, and unless you learn to let go, you cannot move on. If you repeatedly see number patterns of 555, it means the universe is telling you to let go of everything that doesn't serve your purposes. Accept and be open to change in life because new opportunities will soon present themselves. Once you let go of unnecessary burdens, it becomes easier to move ahead. Think of it as decluttering your body, mind and soul.

Ego and fear are associated with the vibrations of 666. If you see this pattern, the universe is conveying the message that your focus has shifted away from the abundance it offers. All the good is instead replaced by fear and a sense of lacking. You don't have to fear this number even though it is often associated with a negative connotation. This pattern is usually a reminder you need to let go of your fears and accept the bright light of the universe.

The number pattern 777 is associated with your feelings and intuition. If you see this pattern, rest easy knowing you are on the right track, and the universe is helping you along. Follow your intuition, trust your gut, and don't worry if there isn't any factual evidence supporting your intuition. Now is the time to meditate, understand yourself better, and go with your gut.

Growth and transformation are the energies resonating from pattern 888. When you see this pattern, it's a message you have gone through a cycle of change and have transformed. Your strength might have been tested recently, but it's a beautiful reminder you are about to receive bountiful rewards.

999 gives out energy vibrations, which bring about a sense of clarity. If your thoughts are cluttered, and you're feeling scared or overwhelmed, this pattern means you need some mental clarity. Now is the time to start afresh and let go of anything that doesn't add value to your life. Meditation and visualization are two tools to do this.

By understanding the meaning of these number codes and deciphering them, you can increase your self-awareness and grow in life. The next time you instinctively feel different groups of numbers, use the information in this chapter to understand whether its energy matches what you feel.

Chapter 6: The Nine-Year Cycle

In numerology, it is believed that every individual goes through nine-year cycles repeatedly. As soon as one nine-year cycle ends, another begins. It consists of nine cycles wherein each cycle lasts for a year, and each year represents something specific. By understanding the nine-year cycle, you get a better insight into what's in store for you. Discovering where you currently stand in a specific cycle helps sneak a peek into what the future holds. To do this, you need to calculate the universal number and your personal year number.

A basic principle of numerology is that all numbers have specific vibrations. Similarly, every year has underlying energy in sync with its corresponding numbers. This subtle energy cannot be overlooked because it affects everyone who lives on this planet. For instance, the universal year number of 2020 is obtained by adding all the individual numbers in it. So, the universal year number is 2+0+2+0, which is 4.

The year 2020 carries with it the stability, manifesting capacities and practicality associated with the energy of 4. In the previous chapters, you were introduced to the simple steps for calculating your life path number. Because of our different life path numbers, how we experience the universal year number varies. You need to consider the effect of the combined vibrations from both the numbers. To get a better insight into this, you need to calculate your personal year number.

Calculate Your Personal Year Number

Calculating your personal year number is simple. As with the life path number, you need your birth date once again to calculate this number. Instead of your birth year, you need to replace it with the universal year to find your personal year number. So, it is the addition of the individual numbers present in your birth month, birthday and the universal year. Here's a simple example to get a better understanding of how to calculate the personal year number. Let's assume that an individual's birth date is 30th February 1980. Now, it is time to calculate the combined total of the birthday and month.

Personal year number = Birthday + birth month + universal year number

The personal year number in the above example is 30+02+2020, which is 3+2+4= 9. If your personal year is 9, it means you are in the final year of a 9-year cycle.

Deciphering the Nine-Year Cycle

Let's delve a little deeper to understand what each of these years truly represents. It will help better show you what the upcoming year will be like. The nine stages of the cycle are beginning, connecting, creating, building, changing, nurturing, re-evaluating, expanding and competing. Once you go through these nine stages, the cycle starts again. In life, every bit of additional information you can get your hands on will be helpful.

The First Year

This is the first year of the starting of a new nine-year cycle. It brings with it a sense of adventure and a promise of something new. It is the starting point of the next cycle of nine years in your life, which comes with its own set of opportunities and challenges. Before you think about acting on your goals, the first step is to clarify them. Now is the time to do this. Hard work is important to move ahead in life, but it is equally important to have a sense of direction and purpose. Since it is the sign of a new beginning, your energy levels will be higher, and you will feel more motivated than you have for a while. You cannot start afresh unless you make some changes. If you cannot make these changes or aren't able to make them, your opportunities might be delayed until the next cycle starts, and you are willing to make the required change. This is one reason why the beginning of the cycle feels like you are about to set on an incredible adventure.

If there is a specific move for a change you have been thinking of making, now is the time to do it. Perhaps you want to start a family, settle down or shift your job. Whatever it is, now is the time to put your plans into action. Set new goals for yourself and start working towards them. It is best you don't think about your past right now and concentrate only on the future. The beginning of the cycle means the previous cycle has ended. The end of the cycle signifies that your problems and disappointments were solved. In their place, new opportunities await you. Be curious and excited for all that life has in store for you this year.

The Second Year

The second year of the cycle might make you feel as if all you are doing is merely waiting in the background. Don't be surprised if you often find yourself in the background; it is a sign of development. Don't concentrate on forcing yourself to move forward but, instead, shift your focus toward personal development. This is a great time to build relationships that will offer benefits and future. It is all about collection and accumulation. During this year, remember there is no scope for aggression. Aggression will become a cause of different problems in life. Waiting in the background takes a lot of patience.

Don't be disheartened if all you do is make small contributions or offer help. Everything that comes your way is an opportunity for growth and development. Don't think of it as anything other than this. It also puts your self-control and emotional sensitivities to the test. Concentrate on improving your skills and abilities to work productively with others. If you are used to working independently or have a lone wolf mentality, this will not be easy. Whatever you do, don't give up on your internal sense of peace and calm. Any nervous tension you experience during this year is temporary, and it will go away. Your emotional sensitivities will be extreme, so this is a great time for you to concentrate on your personal relationships.

The Third Year

The third year of the cycle exudes an energy that's bright, joyous and cheerful. It is an incredibly happy and a social year for you. It not only helps you reconnect with your old friends but also broadens your existing social circle. Besides your social circle, your love life will also blossom. The inclination to live your life to the fullest is at its peak. Well, it would be wise if you slowed down and understood there will be consequences to pay later if you aren't careful. The battle of responsibility seems to have diminished this year, and you will be at your sociable best. Your energy might be a little scattered, and there may be too many commitments to cater to.

This year gives you a chance to enjoy yourself, take a break from the stresses of life and have a good time. It is okay to give in to this temptation to have a good time, but don't forget your goals. This is a great year to work on your creative talents, especially the ones associated with art and verbal skills. Don't get disheartened if the recognition you think you deserve doesn't come easily to you this year. For personal expression and activities, this is a wonderful year, but it doesn't carry the same positivity with your professional life. Unfinished business, rash decisions and a carefree attitude will spell disaster for your career, so concentrate on exercising sufficient self-control. Don't lose sight of your goals because of all the distractions this year brings.

The Fourth Year

The fourth year helps you forget about the frivolity the third you brought into your life. If the previous year wasn't good for your finances, you could compensate for its harmful effects this year. If there is a specific task you need to complete, this year gives you the internal design motivation required to put in the hard work and effort to complete it. It also helps reestablish your self-control instead of getting carried away by the distractions of life. In some ways, it can be a little frustrating when all your hard work doesn't produce the dramatic results you hoped for. It may seem as if you're taking one step forward and two steps back usually. Instead of worrying about the results, concentrate on organizing yourself better. It helps you look at your past and present performance to analyze all that you have achieved. By getting organized, it becomes easier to understand the direction in which you are headed.

The Fifth Year

The fifth year of the cycle brings major life changes. These are to help you to expand your horizon and experience growth. Your set of friends will increase, you will indulge more in social activities and you'll meet a lot of new people. This year brings with it a sense of excitement and adventure. You will also experience more freedom than you did in the previous years. It is time to let go and run free. It gives you the courage required to move away from old routines constructively and work on productivity. If you have been feeling restricted until now, this will help you to seek new directions in life. The only problem with this is your energy might be scattered in different directions. Anything that makes you feel confined will lose its appeal quite quickly.

The Sixth Year

This year is all about home, family, love and responsibility. It is an incredibly personal year where your responsibility might increase. On the plus side, it also deepens the bond you share with your loved ones, whether they are your friends or family members. You might need to make some adjustments in your life or sacrifice a few things for your loved ones. It's more about handling and planning adjustments as you find necessary instead of looking for major compliments. Complete all the projects you might have started in the previous years. You may feel as if you are moving slowly, and you aren't able to see any progress, but on a personal front, matters will improve significantly. Accept living life at a slower pace, and you will enjoy the harmony, love and happiness this year brings.

The Seventh Year

The seventh year encourages self-introspection. It is a perfect time to understand yourself and your desires. So, take a break and reflect on your life. Self-contemplation and introspection give you a chance to break free of all the stresses of daily life and understand yourself. This might not be a year of action, but all the waiting and development you experience will make it worthwhile. Studying, writing and working on integrating your thoughts are some of the best activities suitable for this year. You might seem detached and even aloof but it merely means you are focused on yourself. Use this time and effort to hone and master your skills.

The Eighth Year

After all the self-introspection brought in by the previous year, now it's time to make important changes to your life. The storing of ambition can be felt right now. It's time to make major decisions, work toward bigger achievements. Taking action is what it is all about. After all the self-introspection, it becomes easier to understand the path you should be on and the different changes you need to make to attend goals. Things start going easy for you as long as you recognize opportunities for advancement. Self-confidence and authority are the primary energies associated with the eighth year. Whether it is in your personal or professional life, it's time to pull out all stops and work on your dreams. During this year of your personal cycle, your status and power potential are at their peak. Make the most of it by channeling your inner leader.

The Ninth Year

The end is where we start from, and usually, what we call the beginning in life, is often the end. The ninth year completes a nine-year cycle of your life. It is the year to tie up all the loose ends and reach some conclusions. If there is any unfinished business, there is no time like the present to get on with it. Once you tie up all the loose ends, you can move onto the next nine years of your life without the stress of unresolved matters weighing you down. Remember, whenever a door closes, another one opens. You cannot recognize the new possibilities available in your life if you fail to acknowledge that certain doors are meant to be closed and have been closed.

This year is about facing the reality of your past and how it affects your present right through to the desired course of action needed to create the future you desire. The reality is not just about where you are today or where you wish to be tomorrow. Instead, it's the culmination of everything that happened to you, everyone you have met in life, every feeling you've experienced or denied, and every action or inaction of yours. Who you are today results from your past and everything you have experienced. If there is any aspect of your persona that no longer serves a purpose and merely restricts you to a specific period in time that no longer exists, it's time to let go. Since this year is about completion, complete all your businesses, close all the doors and move on.

You can wake nothing in your life unless necessary endings have taken place. This is the year for reaching out and reflection. You might end up scrutinizing your ideals, ideas and values you may have believed were important in life. Learn to become more involved with others during this year instead of just looking out for yourself.

Chapter 7: The Life Cycle

The journey you want to take in life can be divided into three portions of time known as the major life cycles. These stages represent how you grow and progress in life. The three life cycles are youth, maturity and wisdom. Every major life cycle number comes with its own set of characteristics and traits that will help you grow. The three major life cycles are the areas of development that help fulfill your destiny as you progress through life. Throughout a life cycle, you will learn about the different opportunities and challenges that will come up during your life.

So, how can you calculate your major life cycle number? Well, you just need your birth date for this purpose. The first step is to reduce the corresponding numbers of your birth month, day and year down to three single-digit individual numbers unless they are master numbers. If you have the numbers 11 or 22 as the month, year or day of birth, don't reduce them to 2 or 4. Here is a simple example to get a better understanding of how this number is calculated. Let us calculate the major life cycle numbers for the birth date 11 December 1996. The single-digit numbers or numbers for your birth date are 11, 12 and 7.

The first major life cycle number is known as your youth number.

The second major life cycle number is the cycle of maturity number and this is your month of birth, the maturity number is your day of birth, and the wisdom number is your year of birth.

The third major life cycle number is the cycle of wisdom, the cycle of youth and the cycle of youth numbers.

In the example mentioned above, with the date of birth 11/12/1996 (DD/MM/YYYY format), the major life cycle numbers are as follows.

The first major life cycle number = 3

The second major life cycle number = 11

The third major life cycle number = 7

Let us look at the different age groups through which different life path numbers progress.

Life Path Number 1

- First cycle age- 0- 26 years
- Second cycle age- 27-53 years
- Third cycle age- 54 years and upward

Life Path Number 2

- First cycle age- 0- 25 years
- Second cycle age- 26-52 years
- Third cycle age- 53 years and upward

Life Path Number 3

- First cycle age- 0- 33 years
- Second cycle age- 34-60 years
- Third cycle age- 61 years and upward

Life Path Number 4

- First cycle age- 0-32 years
- Second cycle age- 33-59 years
- Third cycle age- 60 years and upward

Life Path Number 5

- First cycle age- 0-31 years
- Second cycle age- 32-58 years
- Third cycle age- 59 years and upward

Life Path Number 6

- First cycle age- 0-30 years
- Second cycle age- 31-57 years
- Third cycle age- 58 years and upward

Life Path Number 7

- First cycle age- 0-29 years
- Second cycle age- 30-56 years
- Third cycle age- 57 years upward

Life Path Number 8

- First cycle age- 0-28 years
- Second cycle age- 29-55 years
- Third cycle age- 56 years and upward

Life Path Number 9

- First cycle age- 0-27 years
- Second cycle age- 28-54 years
- Third cycle age- 55 years and upward

Life Path Number 11

- First cycle age- 0-26 years
- Second cycle age- 27-53 years
- Third cycle age- 54 and upwards

Life Path Number 22

- First cycle age- 0-32 years
- Second cycle age- 33-59 years
- Third cycle age- 60 years and upward

So, what do each of these life cycle numbers signify for you?

Major Life Cycle Number 1

If your major life cycle number is one, you lean toward independence and love to stand on your own two feet. It gives you a chance to channel your inner leader. This number helps you to walk the path of your choosing and the confidence of trusting your decisions. Throughout your life, the energy vibrations given out by this number make you internally strong, courageous and filled with incredible self-confidence.

You are not bothered by what others think or believe because you know it is not your responsibility to make others happy. You don't have to change yourself because of what others believe, and you understand this truth. This number is a great cycle to start a new venture. Whether it is your personal or professional life, if there is something you want to do, start immediately. From self-employment to starting a business or stepping into a managerial role and advancing your career, this number represents new beginnings.

Major Life Cycle Number 2

The major life cycle number 2 encourages corporation, compassion and sensitivity toward oneself and others. It helps you solve issues diplomatically and learn to make compromises to bring about a sense of harmony to the world. During this, you will be tempted to explore your spiritual and emotional sides to rebalance your life. The universe is now allowing you to tap into your psychic abilities and intuition. This is an ideal time to enter a partnership, stay in a committed relationship, settle down and serve society.

Major Life Cycle Number 3

The major life cycle number 3 gives you a chance to explore your creativity and imagination. This is a period for incredible self-expression. Whether you are expressing yourself artistically, verbally, emotionally or even physically, this year teaches you positive ways of doing this instead of repressing your inner self. You become adept at communicating effectively and efficiently while turning to your creative inclinations. Whether you want to pick up a new hobby, read, paint or draw, write a book or turn to any other artistic avenues, now is the right time.

Major Life Cycle Number 4

The major life cycle number 4 is about working hard and laying down the framework for the future you desire. You value the importance of discipline, dedication, and formal organization while creating something for yourself. It teaches you to persevere, become resilient and overcome any obstacles that come your way while you work on your goals. This is the ideal time to concentrate on your career, renovate your home, commit to a relationship and work on your finances.

Major Life Cycle Number 5

The major life cycle number 5 makes you adaptable and flexible. Number 5 teaches you to value freedom and the need for moderation in all aspects of your life. The desire to explore new places, meet new people, and indulge in new experiences will become your priority during this period. However, while you are busy with all this, don't forget about the bigger picture in life. It is the right time to travel, learn something new, work on self-development and make any significant life changes.

Major Life Cycle Number 6

This number teaches you to take personal responsibility, especially toward your career and relationships with loved ones. You have an inherent desire to be helpful to others and prioritize their needs over your own. During this period, you will learn personal lessons about the importance of love and relationships in life. You also discover the importance of personal boundaries. You finally strike the right balance between playing the roles of a giver and receiver. It is the ideal time to get married, start a family, commit to your relationships, and look for a profession that is service-oriented.

Major Life Cycle Number 7

During this life cycle, you have a desire to peek behind the façade of superficiality. You look for deeper meanings of your desires and are in search of meaningful relationships and things in life. Personal development and delving into your spirituality are the two defining characteristics of this major life cycle. This is the ideal time to focus on yourself and your chosen career. It helps you to be at peace with yourself, and you understand that being alone differs from being lonely. This is the ideal time to improve yourself, develop your intervention, concentrate on your spirituality, and study.

Major Life Cycle Number 8

The major life cycle number 8 encourages you to rethink any undesirable notions about life and finances. Your experience and inherent desire to step into the role of a leader will help progress in your chosen field. You find it easy to stand up for yourself and love taking charge of situations. As long as you put in the required effort and are dedicated to the cause, maintaining healthy relationships in life becomes easier. You attract abundance in all aspects of life. It is the right time to start a business, explore self-employment opportunities, step into the role of a leader, make great strides in your career, and deal with any legal or financial matters.

Major Life Cycle Number 9

This major life cycle number teaches you to understand, accommodate and be compassionate toward yourself and others. It brings with it a broad-mindedness that helps you connect with people from all aspects of life. Forgiving and forgetting is the true representation of this major life cycle. You concentrate on healing yourself and forgiving others for any hurt or grievance they caused in the past. It is the right time to take up a humanitarian cause, serve the community, work on your artistic talents, let go of past trauma and improve relationships with your loved ones.

Major Life Cycle Number 11

This major life cycle number gives you the energy required to increase your consciousness and work on personal development. This is a period of personal growth. As you work on improving and transforming yourself to be your better version, you can pass on this knowledge to others. You finally find inner peace and use it to inspire others. It is the right time to study any form of healing, psychology to counseling, look for a service-oriented profession and work on developing your intuition and spiritual awareness.

Major Life Cycle Number 22

The major life cycle number 22 prompts you to do something that helps others and not just you. Think about where you fit in the bigger picture of life and how you can help others. You want to be of service to the community, your loved ones and the world in general. You might initiate or be engaged in any form of work or service that helps bridge the gap between the real and spiritual realms.

Chapter 8: Charts and Arrows

By now, you have realized numerology is incredibly simple. There's nothing complicated about it. All you need are certain simple calculations, and you can use it to determine your strengths and weaknesses, understand what life has in store and make the most of all the opportunities which come your way. If you are interested in learning more about your numerological chart, let's get started.

The first step toward understanding your numerological chart is through the arrows of Pythagoras. This is a simple and fun way to understand your weaknesses and course trends represented by your date of birth. Every numerological charge doesn't necessarily have arrows. If there are no arrows in your chart, it isn't a bad thing. It's merely a representation of your flexible personality. It means you can easily get accustomed to changing circumstances in life. To draw a numerological chart and find arrows of Pythagoras, the first step is to create a 3 x 3 grid, which will look like this.

In this grid, write down the numbers from 1-9 as follows:

3	6	9
2	5	8
1	4	7

Now, you need to place each number of your birth date in its appropriate square, which was discussed above. If there are any zeros in your birth date, leave them out. For instance, if your birth date is 07.07.1970, the grid will look like this:

To draw a Pythagoras arrow, you need to join three squares that contain numbers or the ones that have no numbers. The arrows can be drawn horizontally, vertically or diagonally. If there are no numbers present in a row, whether it is diagonally, horizontally or vertically, it is known as an empty arrow. In the previous example, the numbers 2, 5, 8, and 4, 5, 6 are absent. 2, 5 8 is the arrow of emotion, and 4, 5, 6 are the arrow of frustration. You will learn more about what the presence or absence of these arrows means later in this chapter. For now, let's look at another example. Let's consider the birthdate 25. 09. 1980. Fill out the corresponding grids with the numbers of this birthdate. When you do this, the grid will look like this.

The grids that can be joined are the ones wherein three numbers are present. There are two full arrows in this example- 2, 5, 8, and 1, 5, and 9.

Are you wondering what a full and empty arrow means? In numerology, a full arrow represents positive traits or strengths, and an empty arrow represents weaknesses. Positive traits or strengths are your natural skills that can be utilized and improved upon to enhance your life's overall quality. An empty arrow shows areas where you are lacking and tend to identify with negative patterns. Understanding all this information makes it easier to take the required action to make the most of what life has to offer.

Meanings of Full Arrows

Arrow of Planning - 1, 2, 3

A full arrow 1, 2, 3 means you are an excellent planner, or your mind is constantly busy thinking about every little detail, is analyzing, and organizing all the information it absorbs and has retained. It is a true representation of your independent personality and your love for personal freedom and independence of thought. These are strengths in your professional life but can become significant obstacles in your relationships. This arrow in an intimate relationship might make you seem aloof, selfish and detached.

Arrow of Willpower - 4, 5, 6

This full arrow in your chart is a representation of your incredible determination and inherent self-control. Whether it is responsibilities, challenges, big projects or anything else that life throws at you, you will be triumphant. You are individualistic and learned to be self-reliant at an early age. Due to this, you might seem a little stubborn in your personal relationships. To ensure that your personal energy level stays well balanced, don't overexert yourself.

Arrow of Activity - 7, 8, 9

If the full arrow of activity is present in your numerology chart, it means physical activity is a significant part of your life. A job that keeps you on your feet and constantly includes some form of movement or other will be ideal for you. You are extroverted and love to interact with others whether or not it's your loved ones or strangers. Since you love to be on the move all the time, taking a break and relaxing might seem difficult for you. Therefore, take a moment, step back and enjoy all that life hasn't supplied for you. If you don't take care of yourself, you will be exhausted, which will cause unnecessary agitation and boredom.

Arrow of Determination - 1, 5, 9

You are a true "go-getter" if the arrow of determination is present in your numerology chart. Some traits you are blessed with are your ambition, patience and persistence. Your desire for these things makes you play well with rigid rules. For working toward your goals and attaining them, you are focused. You don't easily get distracted and have a fine-tuned focus that brings you closer to your goals. This can make you a little rigid and inflexible. Since change is the only constant in life, you need to learn to be more adaptable. It becomes easier to succeed and bring about a sense of harmony to all aspects of your life if you learn to listen to different opinions and become flexible.

Arrow of Practicality - 1, 4, 7

If the arrow of practicality is present in your numerical chart, it means you are skilled in the physical realm. You are well-grounded and have a strong sense of reality, which prevents you from getting distracted by the unimportant details in life. However, you may concentrate too much on the material aspects of life and forget about enjoying the little joys life presents.

Arrow of Emotions - 2, 5, 8

As the name suggests, individuals who have a full arrow of emotions are emotionally balanced and intelligent. Emotional balance is important for your overall well-being and happiness in life. Your emotions regulate your thoughts, thoughts regulate your behavior, and behavior regulates the course of your life. Unless you learn to control your emotions, they will control you. Giving in to your emotions can cause rushed and harsh decisions with significant consequences you need to bear. The great thing about this arrow of emotions is it influences your personal energy to be warm and nurturing. It's quite easy for you to connect with others and form meaningful relationships. All the trials and tests that life has thrown at you have strengthened your character. Using these inherent strengths, you can concentrate on sharing your wisdom to help others.

Arrow of Intellect - 3, 6, 9

Intellect and sophistication are two traits common to individuals with a full arrow of intellect. You are not only in tune with your emotions but those of others too. This tendency makes you empathetic. Once you are empathetic, it becomes easier to understand what others feel and why they feel the way they do. Empathy is an important trait in all aspects of your life, whether it is in your personal or professional life. You are focused on your mental and intellectual development. Besides all those key areas of your life, you need to concentrate on your communication and intimacy.

Arrow of Compassion - 3, 5, 7

The arrow of compassion is also known as the arrow of spirituality. Individuals with this arrow are empathetic. The traits you might associate with it are loyalty, creativity, faithfulness and kindness. Concentrate on gaining a sense of inner balance to grow emotionally and spiritually.

Meanings of Empty Arrows

Now, let's look at what you can understand through the presence of empty arrows in your numerology chart. Empty arrows are often believed to be the embodiment of negative traits. Instead, it will do you good to understand these are certain areas of your life where there is some scope for improvement. When you know where you need to improve yourself, it becomes easier to take the desired course of action.

Arrow of Impracticality - 1, 4, 7

You are a dreamer, and this can make you impractical. It is okay to dream, but it is equally important to understand you need to live in the real realm. Introverts and artists tend to have this arrow. You might have wonderful ideas and incredible goals but might not have the energy required to manifest them into reality. This is one area where you are severely lacking. You cannot achieve your dreams and goals if you don't take the desired action to get there. What is the point of having a clear destination in mind if you aren't sure of the route you need to take? Therefore, don't just concentrate on dreaming big, but also create a solid plan of action to get there. Remember, life is riddled with challenges and obstacles, so plan for them too. Once you do all this, it becomes easier to find the manifestation potential within.

Arrow of Frustration - 4, 5, 6

If this empty arrow is present in your Numerological chart, you probably often find yourself quite frustrated. It's not just frustration with yourself, but with others and even the world in general. Everything and anything seems to trigger you. You also might have the attitude of "My way or the highway." This can create plenty of trouble for you along the way if you are not careful. It is okay to stand up for yourself and be confident about what you believe in, but it is equally important to be flexible in life. Learn to stop being critical of yourself and others. Instead, focus all your energies on inculcating a sense of acceptability. Once you accept yourself, others and life, everything becomes simpler. Don't get overwhelmed, but instead, learn to take control by concentrating on acceptability.

Arrow of Hesitation - 7, 8, 9

There are different instances in life when we hesitate. We hesitate when we don't have the full information to make a decision; we hesitate while trying new things or even with experimentation itself. However, if you find yourself constantly hesitating and not taking any action, it boils down to the arrow of hesitation in your numerological chart. It is essentially a representation of low levels of motivation, determination and a sense of purpose. Without these three things, you cannot get anywhere in life. You might also be at a greater risk of idealizing and having unrealistic expectations. Unrealistic expectations increase the likelihood of disappointment. It also increases the chances of giving up. Therefore, learn to be more action-oriented. Unless you take the first step, you will never know. Concentrate on working toward your goals, keeping your goal small, measurable, attainable, realistic and time-bound. One skill you can benefit from is developing self-discipline. It helps you to tackle any hesitation you experience and makes you a go-getter.

Arrow of Poor Memory - 3, 6, 9

The most prominent effect of the arrow of poor memory often shows up during the early ages of an individual's life. From learning difficulties to trouble concentrating, these are all associated with the arrow of poor memory. You might also notice you tend to get bored quite easily and lose track of things. Therefore, concentrate on working to improve your memory and concentration. The good news is you have complete control over these two aspects of your brain. Instead of concentrating on multitasking, focus solely on one task. You can also try meditation to gain but control over your thoughts.

Arrow of Emotional Sensitivity - 2, 5, 8

The arrow of emotional sensitivity discussed in the previous section brings with it emotional stability and balance. The absence of this arrow makes you overly sensitive to emotions and energies.

This sensitivity is not just to the emotions and energies of others present around you, but the ones present within two. You feel tired and drained when spending time with others. You have a great sense of intuition and are blessed with psychic abilities that others cannot see. The only way to maintain your emotional sensitivity and balance is by developing a strong sense of inner balance. Once the world within you is well balanced, you can finally regain control of your emotions.

Arrow of Skepticism - 3, 5, 7

Skepticism is important in life because it helps you differentiate between reality and fiction. Skepticism is not always about a thing. However, if you deny information that lies outside your comfort zone or conventional norms you are used to, it becomes obstacle. The arrow of skepticism can make you hyper-vigilant, prone to anxiety and even obsessive at times in personal relationships. Therefore, the one thing you need to concentrate on is opening yourself up to new experiences, alternate concepts, multiple perspectives and your opinions of others.

Arrow of Indecision - 1, 5, 9

The arrow of indecision can be challenging, especially when you cannot decide on what you want to do or where you are heading. How can you ever follow through on your decisions if you're not sure of the decision you've already made? Indecision is paralyzing in life. Even though you have a tough time following through with your decisions, you are good at developing new ideas. Work on improving your self-confidence, and this indecision will slowly go away. Instead of getting overwhelmed thinking about taking big risks or following lofty goals, concentrate on smaller steps. Live your life with the idea of one step at a time.

Chapter 9: Calculating Relationships

A common reason people turn to numerology is that they want to learn about their relationship compatibility. Humans are social creatures, and we cannot survive without relationships. One of the most important bonds you will ever form in life is with your special someone. Whether it is the romantic movies or novels, we have all grown up with finding our other half. With numerology, relationship compatibility is determined by calculating the relationship number.

Don't be under any misconception that the lack of compatibility in numerology means the relationship is doomed. Every relationship requires work, and this is the only thing you need to remember.

The relationship number has a special place in numerology. This is better than comparing the separate numerological chart of both partners in the relationship. A relationship number is a single number that encompasses all that the relationship has to offer. Calculating this is quite simple. It is calculated from the life numbers of both partners.

Calculate the life number; you need to add the life path number and the expression number. Once you do this, the sum needs to be reduced to a single-digit number between 1 and 9 unless it's one of the master numbers 11 or 22. In the previous chapter, you were given all the information you need to calculate both these numbers. Calculate the life path number for yourself and your partner. After this, just add them and reduce them to a single-digit between 1- 9 or leave it as 11 or 22 for master numbers.

Here's a simple example to get a better understanding of how the life numbers are calculated. Let us assume that your life path number is 8, and the expression number is 6. So, your life number will be 5 (6 + 8). If your partner's life path number is 7 and the expression number is 9, their life number will be 7 (7 + 9). The final step is to add your life number to that of your partners. So, you will end up with relationship number 3 (5+7). This number is unique to your relationship. Now let's look at interpreting each of these relationship numbers.

Relationship Number 1

If you and your partner have something to focus on, this relationship will thrive and prosper. Ambitions and goals are key to this relationship. Maybe you have plans to shift to an exotic location, start a family together, build your home or maybe even a business. Both partners in this relationship have incredible skills, and when you put them together, it enhances what you each can achieve individually. You are the ultimate power couple and will inspire others. If you think your relationship is struggling, you probably have both lost your common purpose and are slowly drifting away from each other. Pump more energy into this relationship, and it will prosper again. Think about starting something new together and make sure you are both passionate about it. It will help rekindle the fire, sparks and passion in the relationship. This newfound passion will help build a thriving partnership that pushes you toward a common goal.

Relationship Number 2

Communication is the most important aspect of a relationship defined by number two. It doesn't matter whether you are both expressive as individuals, but it is important for the health of your relationship. You can use each other's support system to develop better communication skills. It also makes it easier to be sensitive and caring toward one another. The purpose of this relationship is not to balance out any qualities or traits you possess as individuals. Instead, it's about looking for your inner sense of balance.

If your relationship is going through a rough patch right now, it will pass. In the meanwhile, you both need to make a conscious effort and create more time and space for one another. Learn to listen and connect with no judgments. Keep an open heart and mind with your partner. Or maybe you have both forgotten what it means to compromise. A relationship is riddled with compromises. A compromise doesn't mean you are giving up on something you love. Instead, it's merely about making certain adjustments for the sake of love and your relationship. The relationship is not about a single individual but instead, it is about both of you. It is a partnership.

Relationship Number 3

Working and creating together is what makes this relationship exciting. Don't restrict your inner child and let it come out sometimes. This relationship needs to be exciting, playful and therefore you both need to be expressive. This is important if you both have other responsibilities and jobs that take away your inner sense of freedom and inhibition. Tune into your carefree nature, and watch your relationship grow. Social settings or any other situations that let you live life to the fullest are the key to a happy and successful relationship influenced by number 3.

If you have lost this element of fun, your relationship can struggle. Therefore, learn to bring in more energy and don't get caught in the mundane routines. Let go of your inhibitions, be spontaneous and permit yourself to be silly.

Relationship Number 4

If you and your partner are concentrating on building a future together, this relationship will be the best thing that's happened to you. Staying grounded and feeling organized are two things quite essential for this relationship. Adding routines and having a general sense of direction will be good for you both. Even if both your life path numbers don't adhere to these conditions, this is what the future of your relationship relies on. Your solid and stable partnership is an inspiration to others, and it is admirable.

If you have both become ungrounded, this relationship will struggle a little. Focus more on the little details of the life you spend together. Delegate responsibilities, share duties, and work out the practicalities of your personal life together. If this firm rooting is absent, your relationship will not survive.

Relationship Number 5

Exploring the wonders of life is what keeps this relationship alive. Every turn of the relationship needs to feel exciting and new. If you and your partner are spontaneous and a little carefree, this partnership will be rewarding. It also means you both need to give each other plenty of personal space while making time for adventures together. Organize your life so you can add some diversity to it while keeping things exciting without forgetting about responsibilities. Don't get caught up in the practicalities of life and forget to smell the roses once in a while. Learn to grow and stay together without compromising on your freedom.

If your life gets mundane, the relationship will become stale. There are different activities you can indulge in to rekindle the energy of five into your relationship. Something as simple as a date night or an impromptu getaway will work wonders. Add a touch of variety, and your relationship will be as good as new again.

Relationship Number 6

In a healthy, lasting and strong relationship, there needs to be a sense of security. You are your partner sanctuary, and vice versa. Unless this element exists in your relationship, it cannot evolve. Therefore, your relationship needs to give out safe and positive energy. In this wonderful space you are both creating together, there's nothing you cannot achieve together. It also gives you a chance to express your creative gifts with no worries, fears or anxiety. The energy given out by you as a couple is something that attracts many people to your house. The party never ends at your house.

If you do not nurture this relationship, it will wither away. Therefore, be careful. It is important to socialize with others, but it is equally important to spend time with each other. If your schedule is getting quite hectic, take a break, and make time and space for each other. After all, how can a relationship survive if both partners are not together? Make it a point it is an equal partnership. One cannot be the receiver and the other the nurturer. Once you attain this equilibrium in the relationship and make sure you are both being cared for, your relationship will become strong. Taking care of each other is simple. Perhaps you can cook your partner's favorite meal, go to their favorite restaurant, or maybe even watch a movie you both love together. It's always about the gestures you make that help the partnership to last and be fulfilling.

Relationship Number 7

Relationship number 7 signifies that the bond between the partners needs to be deep. Superficiality is not a sign of a healthy or lasting relationship. In this relationship, you both need to feel like you are on a quest to find the deeper meaning of life. By working on each other's knowledge and looking for creative and authentic ways to live life, you will try to prosper together as a couple. You both love spending time together with no distractions. This helps explore your lives together and see it is molded according to your desires.

A common challenge this relationship number faces is from an external source. If societal norms and expectations of your loved ones become restrictive or cumbersome, your relationship will struggle. Therefore, it's time to get away from all this. Let go of external expectations and instead concentrate on each other and what you both desire. Sit down and have an open and honest conversation about where you want the relationship to head. When you work together as a team, you will both be inspired to do better individually.

Relationship Number 8

There is a free flow of wealth and power in this relationship. It almost feels as if you're both building an empire together. However, there must always be a balance of power between the partners. If not, the relationship will struggle a little. Number 8 is associated with balance. However, its energy might also represent rising and fall. Therefore, your relationship will go through several stages and cycles. The only thing that matters is you are both in it together and don't let go of each other. These ups and downs are not anyone's fault, and this is the manifestation of the energy associated with the number 8.

The simplest way to rebalance and re-energize your relationship is by addressing any imbalances in your partnership. Don't worry about who is in charge of what. Instead, learn to take responsibility for things together. If not, the responsibilities can be equally divided out. Once you do this, you can both work together as a team to build the empire you desire.

Relationship Number 9

Since relationship number 9 is associated with spirituality, you will both have an inherent desire to be of service to others. At times, the relationship might feel as if it is operating on a higher plane of reality that isn't confined by the restrictions of the physical realm. Whether it does contribute to a charity you are passionate about or offering helpful advice, you will both do it gladly. However, ensure that you have sufficient energy for each other. After all, the relationship is about you and not all the good you do for others. Look at the bigger picture, but it is equally important to look at your relationship. If you are both too caught up and doing your bit for society, this relationship can struggle a little. Instead, shift your focus inwards and toward your relationship. What can you do for each other? What do you bring to the table? How can you help your relationship? These are questions you both need to answer together.

Relationship Number 11

Since master number 11 is deeply rooted in spirituality, if both partners are on a spiritual journey together, the relationship will thrive. As for relationship number 2, you both need to communicate effectively. Besides communication, there needs to be mutual care, empathy and sensitivity. Understand that the purpose of your relationship is not true to balance each other's traits but to gain a sense of inner balance. Once you are both at peace, the relationship will prosper. Being energetic and interested in spiritual awakening comes with its own set of challenges. So, you both need to brace yourselves and get through all the hurdles that come your way because the relationship is truly worth it. The number 11 represents two pillars that stand strong together. You are both equals in the relationship. The wonderful insights, coupled with your deep integration, will be helpful for both of you. Since it is a highly spiritual number, you both need to stay grounded in the physical realm and not get carried away full stock.

Relationship Number 22

This relationship excels when both the partners work together to create a visionary future together. It essentially means you both need to accept your gift and work on creating specific routines. This helps your relationship stay organized and grounded. These are two trades that appeal to both of you. Once you have a solid base, it becomes easy to communicate effectively and efficiently. You can also share your brilliant plans for creating a wonderful future together. Individuals with relationship number 22 have incredible potential to manifest great things that will help this world become a better place.

If there are any issues in your relationship, the only aspect you need to concentrate on is communication. Once you both communicate openly, honestly and from a deeper place, most of your issues will subside. This is a powerful master number, and you should never isolate yourself from each other. Remember, you are both a unit and need to work together. Don't get too carried away with spirituality and take time for yourselves.

Chapter 10: Ayurveda and Numerology

Ayurveda is a Sanskrit term, which translates to "knowledge of life." When people talk about Ayurveda, they think of alternative medicine. Well, Ayurveda is so much more than just medicine. It is a way of life and an healthy one at that. For over 5000 years, the system has been actively used in India. It includes a variety of lifestyle practices such as yoga, dietary changes, meditation, herbal remedies and massages to improve one's overall health and prevent or treat illnesses. This is a holistic medicine that views the body and mind as a single component. Unlike western medicine that tries to look for a universal treatment for a problem, Ayurveda believes every individual is unique. Instead of dealing with only the physical ailments or problems an individual has, Ayurveda improves one's overall health and wellbeing.

Ayurvedic philosophy is based on the universal law of nature about balance. This is one reason why Ayurveda helps balance your external and internal wellbeing.

There are five basic elements - water, earth, fire, air, and space that constantly interact with us and each other form of creation. These elements are categorized into three primary types of energy and principles that apply to everything, and everyone present in this world. These three components or doshas are known as Vata, Pitta and Kapha. These doshas are not only associated with the primary elements of nature but all our bodily functions too.

Kapha denotes water and earth. It represents our immune system and the physical structure of the human body. Even our emotional responses, such as our ability to love, forgive, and stay calm are governed by Kapha.

Vatta denotes air and space. Our joints, muscles, heartbeat and breathing are all governed by this component of the universe. It is also responsible for governing our nervous system and regulating pain and anxiety.

Pitta denotes fire and water. This element governs important bodily functions such as intelligence, metabolism, digestion and skin color. It is also responsible for governing certain powerful emotions such as hatred and jealousy.

These three doshas are determined at a time of birth and relate to our overall personality and basic physical makeup. For instance, the Kapha body structure is well developed and usually bigger than Vatta's small and thin build or the pitta's medium muscular build. For once overall wellbeing, all these three doshas need to be balanced in your body. Any imbalance in these shows results in illnesses and other conditions which harm our health. Ayurvedic practices are good for maintaining your overall health, improving flexibility, strengthening your body and mind, enhancing your stamina, reducing stress and even tackling other harmful conditions such as arthritis, asthma and high blood pressure.

Did you know there are eight branches in Ayurveda? It includes pediatrics, internal medicine, ear, nose and throat treatment, surgery, psychiatry, toxicology, fertility and conception therapy, geriatrics and rejuvenation. Besides all this, Ayurveda offers a wonderful cleansing protocol termed Panchakarma. It uses five therapies to help your body let go of all the toxins stored within its tissues and muscles while rebalancing doshas. Ayurveda is based on the principle of balance. It's believed everything in the universe has its own specific vibration. This theory is similar to the belief in numerology.

Vedic Numerology

Vedas are ancient Indian texts of knowledge and wisdom on different topics written thousands of years ago. Until now, you were introduced to the concept of western numerology. There is one other branch of numerology, which is vastly studied, and it is Vedic numerology. Vedic numerology uses numbers to study and get a better understanding of human behavior, temperament, natural disposition, destiny, sexuality, intelligence and so on. This form of numerology stems from Samkhya philosophy and Vedic rituals symbolism. Samkhya means numbers, and it forms the basis for Ayurveda and yoga too. It is closely related to the different patterns present in nature, the composition and construction of the human body, and the importance and role of different organs present. It seeks to understand the numbers hidden in objects, living beings and different patterns that somehow shape human personality.

One of the most important differences between Vedic and western numerology is associated with numeral representations. In Vedic numerology, it's believed that every number is associated with specific deities. According to Vedic teachings, deities are the representation of different planets. There are nine numbers in Vedic numerology, and 9 corresponding deities or planets represent them.

Numerology plays an important role in Hinduism, even today. Certain days of the year are considered auspicious, while some are inauspicious. Different numbers bring with them the influence of different planets. Certain rituals and ceremonies such as marriage, naming ceremony of a newborn, starting a business venture, and so on are performed at a specific time on a given day. In Vedic tradition, astronomy and astrology are closely related. There are patterns in everything, and numbers form these patterns. Numbers by themselves hold a special place in Vedic philosophies. For instance, the rosary beads used for repeating mantras have 108 beads. The distance between the sun and the earth is 108 times the Sun's diameter. Therefore, the number 108 is believed to be the key to attaining spiritual enlightenment.

There is as such no importance for zero in numerology. This number by itself has no value. Its placement determines its value. Even though it adds no value to numerological calculations, it holds special significance in numerology. Zero is known as Shoonya in Sanskrit. It is believed to symbolize the beginning and the end. It is the embodiment of nothingness and the void. Everything comes from Shoonya and goes back to Shoonya in the end.

Number 1

It is associated with the sun. Individuals with this number have a strong sense of individuality, masculine energy, they love to be in control and love their personal freedom. They are also intelligent, bright and love all the comforts and luxuries of life.

Number 2

It is associated with the moon. Individuals with this number are emotional, intuitive, gentle, nurturing and peace-loving. Their personalities are flexible and attractive.

Number 3

It is associated with the planet Jupiter. Individuals with this number are energetic, spiritual, disciplined and strongly built. They prefer rational thinking, work on acquiring more knowledge and are dutiful.

Number 4

It is associated with the planet Rahu. Individuals with this number are often stubborn, moody, short-tempered, impulsive and unpredictable. They can also be secretive and selfish to a great extent.

Number 5

It is associated with the planet Mercury. Individuals with this number have a child-like nature playful, free-spirited, adaptable and sensitive. They are also logical, bright and have progressive thinking.

Number 6

It is associated with the planet Venus. Individuals with this number are sensuous, friendly, artistic, soft-spoken and well organized. The gentle nature, coupled with creativity and tact, makes them approachable.

Number 7

It is associated with the planet Ketu. Individuals with this number are insightful, dreamy, indecisive and intuitive. They believe in mysticism, are drawn to religions and are sentimental and highly insightful. They also love nature, and everything associated with it.

Number 8

It is associated with the planet Saturn. Individuals with this number are strong-willed, introverted, thoughtful, caring and protective. They are hardworking, wise and subservient.

Number 9

It is associated with the planet Mars. Individuals ruled by the planet Mars are short-tempered, have a dominating personality, are aggressive, strong and have strong leadership traits. Don't let their harsh exterior fool you because they're quite soft on the inside.

All the different qualities corresponding to the planetary deities must never be taken in that literary sense because they manifest in humans in varying degrees. According to Vedic philosophy, every human being is a unique distinct destiny and karma. Therefore, several factors need to be considered while determining the primary characteristics and traits, along with the destiny of individuals. In Vedic numerology, only the numbers matter. Other factors that are important in astrology, such as planetary positions, don't matter here.

The psychic number or the birth number is calculated based on the birth day. If the number is greater than 9, they need to be reduced to a single digit. The psychic number plays an important role in shaping your overall personality and behavior. It also influences all the choices you make in life, whether about the food you wish to eat or the profession you choose and the goals you set and other personal relationships. Because every number is associated with a planetary deity, the qualities associated with the corresponding deity manifest in individuals born under the specific number.

The destiny number is calculated by summing up all the individual digits present in your full date of birth. So, it is important because it influences the course of your life and destiny too. Your destiny combines your past karma and any latent impressions leftover from your previous birth. This number becomes especially important after the age of 35. By adding the numerological value of all the letters in your birth name, you will arrive at your name number. While doing this, there is a significant difference between western and Vedic numerology. Every alphabet is assigned a value between the numbers one and eight. Number 9 is excluded from calculations present in the Vedic square because adding it to any other number does not alter the number's primary value. For instance, 3 + 9 = 12 or 3, 2+9 = 11 or 2, 1+9= 10 or 1.

You might recall from the previous chapters based on calculations of your full name; western astrology concentrates only on the full birth name, excluding any suffixes. In Vedic astrology, you can calculate the name number for your nicknames and even other aliases. If you are usually referred to by your last name at work, the number will be based on your last name to determine your work life. If you are known by your nickname at home, your home life is determined by the number culminating from the sum of your nickname and so on. The name number per se exudes little influence on your destiny, but it influences your birth number and general behavior in life.

A primary difference between Vedic numerology and western numerology is in the treatment of master numbers such as 11 and 22. In Vedic numerology, this concept does not exist. For instance, if the sum of one's destiny number, life path number, or any other number results in 11 or 22, it is further converted to a single digit that makes it 2 or 4. Everything in Vedic numerology is converted to a single digit. For instance, if the birthdate is 03/06/2000, the life number will be 2(3 + 6 + 2 = 11). The concept of master numbers doesn't exist in Vedic numerology.

There is an alternate practice for dealing with master numbers 11 and 22. If an individual's number is 11, the qualities associated with number 1 are prominent and strong in him.

Chapter 11: Astro-Numerology

Both Astrology and Numerology have existed as metaphysical sciences for centuries and have been used by curious minds to get a better insight into their own lives and the lives of others. Some intrepid exponents of these fields have even made accurate predictions about future events.

Astrology has its roots dating to the second millennium BCE and can be traced to Babylon, Mesopotamia from where it spread to Egypt, Ancient Greece, Rome and gradually to Europe and from there to Arabia. Astrology is the study of the locations and movements of celestial bodies within the solar system. Based on this, astrologers prepare your natal or birth chart, which uses complicated calculations derived from the angles, degrees, house and positions of the Sun, Moon, and other relevant stars at the time of your birth to prepare a graphical chart using the sectors of a 360-degree circle.

Numerology, on the other hand, is a relatively modern discipline and is generally attributed to being conceptualized by the Greek philosopher and mathematician Pythagoras, who lived in the fifth century BCE. (Yes, the very same Pythagoras who came up with the Pythagoras Theorem, you studied in school). Pythagoras believed that each object in the universe is associated with a number, each of which has its significance. This theory was subsequently endorsed by Einstein, who believed that each number vibrates differently and can attract both negative and positive energies and thereby affect your personality and events in life. The system propounded by Pythagoras and Einstein has been expanded endlessly in modern times and has eventually been shaped into the concepts of numerology as we know it today,

Numerology consists of five core numbers, which are the birthday, life path, personality expression and Zodiac. Of these, the most common is the "Life Path Number". To know your Life Path Number, all you require is your birthdate. You need to add the individual digits of your birth date together so that all two or over two-digit numbers are added until they result in a single-digit number. For example, let us consider the birth date, 19 June 1970 (19/6/1970).

The date of 19 will be $1 + 9$, resulting in 10, which will be added as $1 + 0 = 1$.

The month of June or 6 is all alone, so it will remain as 6.

The last number will be the year of birth - 1970, which will be added as $1 + 9 + 7 + 0 = 17$, which will further result in $1 + 7 = 8$.

The sum of the above date/month/year will add up to $(1 + 6 + 8) = 15$, which further leaves us with $1 + 5 = 6$.

So, the Life Path Number is 6.

The above may seem pretty simple; however, there is a catch! Whenever a date, month of the year add up to 11 or 22, you do not reduce them further to single-digit numbers but retain them as they are because 11 and 22 are "master numbers" with special significance.

What does 6 as the Life Path Number signify?

Strengths of Life Path No 6: An impassioned speaker/activist, bestowed with curiosity and compassion. Ideal occupations are lawyers, orators, therapists or social services.

Challenges of Life Path Number 6: Difficulty Being Consistent

Characteristics of the Zodiac Sign – Gemini

Gemini is considered the chameleon of the Zodiac because of their ability to display different facets of themselves to the world and adapt and blend with different types of people depending on the vibes other people send out. They are also considered highly intelligent individuals who can sway people in their favor by their quick decision-making ability.

Therefore, the Life Path Number of 6 seems to indicate that the individual is a passionate activist who wishes to contribute to society and loves convincing others via his arguments. They can get along with people with different views and easily adapt themselves to any social setting. When the Life Path Number is correlated with the Zodiac, you will realize that the readings reinforce each other to give a more comprehensive picture of who you are.

An individual's Life Path Number may also list out characteristics attributed to other zodiac signs, which may probably signal the existence of an astrological alter ego. This seems very probable considering that each life path number is ruled by a specific celestial body of the solar system just like in astrology.

Once you have worked out your Life Path Number, discover which planet rules your destiny and the characteristics of your astrological alter ego.

Number 1 - Ruled by The Sun

Astrology Alter Ego: Leo

Number 1 people are always leaders, like the king of the zodiac – Leo, the lion.

Others look up to you, you are assertive and a trendsetter, whether in terms of fashion or with your bold, unique perspective on current affairs. You always take the lead, and others step in behind you.

Number 2 - Ruled by The Moon

Astrology Alter Ego: Cancer

As under the zodiac sign of Cancer, the Moon rules number two using numerology. If you are ruled by number 2, you will likely be a balanced, fair, caring and open-minded person who often acts as a mediator in feuds in your friend circle. You are the "go-to" guy who offers a patient listening to your friends and siblings and helps them sort out their issues. You are very sincere and sensitive and very affected by seeing others in distress.

Number 3 - Ruling Planet: Jupiter

Astrology Alter Ego: Sagittarius and Pisces

You are filled with creativity, imagination and energy. Mostly your passion will lie in one of the artistic disciplines, painting, writing, acting, dancing, creation, etc.

Sagittarius confers on you the ability to lucidly express your views and adapt to varied situations and people, whereas emotional sensitivity and creativity are gifts from Pisces. You are also likely to be very determined and resolute about your principles and goals.

Number 4 - Ruling Planet: Uranus

Astrology Alter Ego: Aquarius

You are likely to be unique and innovative, one who lives life by his own rules. You are not a blind follower of people, but one who is an independent thinker who makes his own decisions. You are spiritual and one who is equally comfortable amidst nature or with some of his numerous pals. You have the eye to take something simple and transform it into something grander by your signature touch. You are also diligent and have a strong intuition that helps you escape unpleasant situations.

Number 5 - Ruling Planet: Mercury

Astrology Alter Ego: Gemini, Virgo

You are intelligent, always ready with a one-liner and a witty comeback. You are the one who will always come up with a solution to an issue. Your zodiac alter ego Gemini blesses you with your enthusiastic nature and high spirits, whereas the credit for your intellect and wit should be attributed to Virgo. You are also unexpectedly grounded and despite your vivacious and free-spirited nature, you prefer to stick to familiar people and places in your life.

Number 6 - Ruling Planet: Venus

Astrology Alter Ego: Taurus, Libra

Individuals ruled by number 7 are hopeless lovers like most Taureans. They are enchanted by beauty, sensuality and romance and are always aspiring for the finer things in life.

Your easygoing and composed personality is a characteristic gifted to you by your zodiac counterpart Libra. You are a very persistent individual who follows every goal with tenacity. The most striking attribute in you is your exquisite taste.

Number 7 - Ruling Planet: Neptune

Astrology Alter Ego: Pisces

You are highly spiritual, like your ruling planet Neptune and your zodiac alter-ego Pisces. You love solitude and activities where you have the opportunity to read, research and self-reflection. You are intelligent and very knowledgeable but never use your mental facilities to impress others. You are always in support of the underdog or those who are misunderstood. You have a natural ability to understand others. Unfortunately, very few people can grasp your views on a deeper level.

Number 8 - Ruling Planet: Saturn

Astrology Alter Ego: Capricorn

You are most probably ambitious but have a soft and kind inner core under your indifferent exterior. You are very rigid and uncomfortable exploring new things. You are very sincere and dedicated. Like your zodiac counterpart Capricorn, you want balance and steadiness in your life. Emotional and financial security are very important for you in life.

Number 9 - Ruling Planet: Mars

Astrology Alter Ego: Aries, Scorpio

If ruled by number 9, you are a natural leader, confident, with a strong personality and opinion. Unfortunately, your humanitarian spirit of exploring and creating to benefit others rarely is perceived by others. You are impulsive and don't mind following your whims, even if it means going solo.

What is Astro-Numerology and what is the relation to each other?

When considered together, we realize there is a lot more in common between Astrology and Numerology than previously thought. Both rely heavily on mathematics and complex calculations to infer and explain the significance of the symbols associated with each discipline. While knowledge of mathematics and numbers is a prerequisite for preparing and interpreting a natal or birth chart, an additional understanding of planets and celestial bodies' influence enhances a numerologist's insight and interpretation of his readings. Therefore, when applied in conjunction, both astrology and numerology integrate into a fairly new field – Astro-Numerology. Astro-numerologists, whose readings are based on both astrology and numerology, have a broader picture than others who use one or the other.

Do you wonder how understanding the astro-numerology chart will help you to gain self-awareness? Your natal chart is a concise assessment of your desires, aptitudes, dreams and your life's mission. It shows you where you stand in life, the highest potential you can reach, and what you need to do to attain that potential. The five core numbers in numerology give you crucial knowledge about your purpose in life, your abilities and your inclinations. If you refer to your Astro-numerological chart when making an important decision, you can consider your strengths, inclinations, weaknesses and your purpose in life. The subsequent decision you make will be an informed one in line with the numbers, resulting in the most favorable outcome in life.

Most people who lack conviction and are not sure of their purpose in life, often live their lives as per the dictates of others or merely doing what they consider their obligations in life. Such people fail to achieve their true dharma or purpose in life and remain uncontended all their lives, chasing the dreams of others rather than their own. However, if you know your life's mission and have a strong sense of self and awareness about what you are capable of, you will not be swayed by what people say or think about you. Your self-confidence will not be affected by the labels that people attempt to slap on you because your conviction in yourself will help you overcome these obstacles and criticisms. What you think and assume becomes a reality for you. For example, even if you had the inclination and the talent to be a great artist, but you are not convinced of your ability or are dissuaded by others, you cannot succeed or find satisfaction in your life's calling. However, if backed by the data from your natal chart, and you are convinced of your artistic ability, you will be motivated to devote more attention to your passion with gusto. In this manner, awareness about numerology can help you take advantage of your strengths and achieve greater self-awareness, confidence and success, leading eventually to self-contentment and fulfillment in life.

If you have ever felt disconnected from your zodiac sign or wish to get a deeper insight into what the stars foretell, Astro-Numerology may probably have the answer to your questions. Give it a try!

Chapter 12: Tarot and Numerology

Tarot is a study of cards that are used to predict the future. Numerology is the study of energy vibrations associated with specific numbers and their connectivity. The philosophy of both these concepts dates to thousands of years, yet they are connected. The tarot deck contains 78 cards, and each card has its own meanings, symbolism and imagery. Don't get worried that you have to learn about all the 78 cards. Once you go through the information in this section, you will discover that understanding tarot is simple. These 78 cards are divided into two major categories known as Minor Arcana and Major Arcana. The Major Arcana includes 22 cards that represent significant life lessons, including spiritual ones. The other cards are the Minor Arcana and are divided into four suits of 14 cards each.

In a tarot reading, the properties of the cards suit, imagery and life lessons are combined to understand whether the individual is on the path toward self-discovery and self-development or not. It also helps ascertain if there are any possible challenges and hurdles the individual needs to overcome while working toward their goals. Tarot can be used to understand what fortune the future has in store for you or what happened in the past. Others think of it as a tool for self-reflection.

Major Arcana Cards

The significant archetypal themes in life are associated with the Major Arcana cards. Whether it is about karmic influences or life lessons, you can know more about them with Major Arcana cards. All the significant changes and transformations in life, whether good or bad, can be understood by using these cards. They are also known as trump cards. They often set the tone for a tarot reading because all the other cards will reflect the core Major Arcana cards' dominant energy.

The Major Arcana cards consist of 21 numbered cards and one unnumbered card (the fool), and they are as follows.

- The fool
- The magician
- The high priestess
- The Empress
- The emperor
- The hierophant
- The lovers
- The chariot
- Strength (known as Justice in some decks)
- The home at
- Wheel of fortune
- Justice (known as Strength in some decks)
- The hangman
- Death

- Temperance
- The devil
- The tower
- The star
- The moon
- The sun
- Judgment
- The world

Now, let's learn more about these Major Arcana cards.

The Fool

The fool is the only unnumbered card in the tarot deck. It symbolizes zero. By understanding what this card means, you understand the true power of zero. Zero is a circle, which represents totality. There is no beginning and no end to this. It is the zone of emptiness, nothingness and openness. It is purity and is defined by absence.

The Magician

The magician is a representation of creativity, the mind and attraction. Zero is nothingness, and one is about creation. Therefore, the first card of the tarot deck is where manifestation starts. One is the starting point and the first number defined. It is always about singular focus and an individual act. It can also be interpreted as of one mind and committing yourself to a specific subject without letting your attention get diverted.

The High Priestess

One is an individual, and this attracts another, which is the high priestess or number two. It is all about balance. The high priestess balances nature's opposing forces: intuition and rationality, hidden and revealed meanings, and the inner and outer worlds. It's about polarity and unity. It means two individuals are coming together to form a complete persona. Two is about expansion. This might suggest the saying two heads are better than one. Whether it is an idea or a business venture, it symbolizes the start of something new and exciting.

The Empress

A third factor that breaks the tools' polarity is introduced, and this is where the Empress steps into the picture. She is a representation of expansion and abundance. This expresses all the effort you made in the previous number. Since you've worked on attracting resources and abundance into your life along with progress, it is time to set certain limits and boundaries. Boundaries, structure and protection are important to safeguard your resources and make the most of them. If you have amassed wealth, the next step is to define what you want to do with that and how you decide.

The Emperor

The boundaries mentioned in the previous step can be set with this number. The Emperor is the representation of protection and strength. He's the overseer and the Guardian of all your resources and keeps them in order. This is the point of balance in the tarot. Nothing in life can exist if it isn't balanced. The energy given out by 2's is balanced by 4.

The Hierophant

This card is the representation of growth and challenge. If twos are the legs of wood and 4 is the table that rests on them, 5 is the challenger conflict, which senses shakes in the table. Complacency kills growth and development. You cannot grow in life without conflicts, and this is where the hierophant steps into the picture. Instead of getting too used to comforts, the hierophant challenges you to live up to higher standards and strive for something better. Five is also associated with the pentacles of Minor Arcana suits. Therefore, it is the combination of four important elements - water, fire, air and earth. Even though this card is viewed as a disruption, it ushers in growth.

The Lovers

The sixth card of the Major Arcana is the lovers. It is all about balance and harmony. If there is an excess disruption in your life, everything becomes chaotic, and there is another need for balance. The Lovers card brings this balance. It is considered a mystical number that is a true embodiment of the union between the divine feminine and masculine energies.

The Chariot

The seventh card of the Major Arcana deck is a representation of healing, spirituality and growth. This number awakens any dormant desires present within. It challenges you to pursue your goals and suggest more to life than you are looking at. It encourages you to ask important questions to make the required changes to move ahead in life. Therefore, this is the card that makes you chase your dreams. However, before you do that, it's time for a little self-introspection. Self-introspection helps you understand what you want and the reasons for the same. Once you know the destination, it becomes easier to plan the required course of action.

Strength (Also Known as Justice in Some Decks)

This card is all about balance and Infinity. Given its shape, it signifies Infinity. It is hard to determine where the number 8 starts and ends. It conveys the message that in life, everything always comes to a full circle. If it doesn't, it means there is more in store for you. It is also associated with stability, a secure foundation and abundance. In some interpretations, it is believed to be the fall of the year. Number 2 is about unity and polarity, while 4 is about protection, sturdiness and stability. Since number 8 is the combination of 2 multiplied 4, all these wonderful traits are welcome into your life by it.

The Hermit

The hermit is representative of expansion and advancement. It is also believed to be a number associated with mysticism. Since 3 represents mysticism and 9 is 3 * 3, its significance further intensified. This card encourages you to set out on a powerful journey where transformation is the goal. It helps you advance spiritually and even ideologically. By channeling your inner power, it enables you to set out on a unique path. It's commonly misunderstood that the hermit is a representation of loneliness. Instead, the hermit teaches you to be at peace with yourself. Being alone differs from loneliness. By understanding this difference, it becomes easier to tread on the path less traveled in life.

Wheel of Fortune

The wheel of fortune is a representation of completion and renewal. If one is the beginning, 10 is completion. Ten is nothing but a combination of one and zero. These are two powerful numbers. When the fool and the magician come together, it becomes the wheel of fortune. It also suggests nothing is impossible if this card shows up in your deck.

You don't have to learn about all the 22 Major Arcana cards. Instead, learning about the first ten cards will do for now. The information you obtain from the single-digit Major Arcana cards can be used to understand the double-digit ones. To keep things simple, merely add the numbers on the double-digit cards and reduce them to a single digit. Here is a simple example to clarify things.

The Star is the 17th Major Arcana card. When you reduce it to a single digit, you get 8. The 8th Major Arcana card is strength. While you experiment with different cards, you will notice certain interconnections between them. For instance, the imagery of the Lovers card is like the devil card. The devil card is believed to be the inverse of the Lovers card. Well, this isn't a coincidence. The Lovers card is the 6th Major Arcana card, and the devil is the 15th.

This shows the numerical link between different cards in tarot. When the Lovers card is imbalanced, it becomes the devil card.

Minor Arcana Cards

There are 56 Minor Arcana cards used to understand more about one's trials and tribulations daily. Even though the word minor is used to describe these cards, it doesn't mean they have no effect on your life. It merely means they refer to the instances and happening in your daily life. To gain more insight into your current situation, understand any obstacle standing in your way and work on manifesting your goals, it's important to understand your Minor Arcana tarot cards. The influence associated with the Minor Arcana is believed to be temporary. It essentially means as you progress through life, the energy they give changes based on the actions you take.

A tarot reading of Minor Arcana cards helps you understand what is happening in your life right now. It gives a better insight into how the happenings of your daily life are influencing you. These offer insight into your thoughts, emotions, interactions with others and experiences as you go through life. The previous section mentioned that Major Arcana helps you understand the primary life lesson you are learning right now. The Minor Arcana cards will show the situation you are dealing with right now that's helping you learn the lesson. Even though the situation is temporary, it has immense potential to alter the course of your life.

The four suits of Minor Arcana cards are as follows.

The Suit of Wands

It represents your energy levels, passion and motivation. In a tarot reading, these cards appear when you want to know about your life purpose, contact your spirituality or work on new ideas. The element they are associated with is fire.

The Suit of Swords

In your words, actions and thoughts these are represented by the suit of swords. If these cards show up in a tarot reading, it is a sign you need to work on communicating all your wonderful ideas when you want to assert your independence and power and while making decisions. The element they are associated with is air.

The Suit of Cups

Your intuition, creativity, feelings and emotions are represented by the suit of cups. During a tarot reading about your emotional connection and relationships with yourself and others around you, these cards will come up. The element they are associated with is water.

The Suit of Pentacles

A suit of pentacles is the embodiment of all your material possessions, your finances and your career. Any tarot reading associated with your career or work and finances will include the suit of pentacles. The element they are associated with is earth.

Each of these four suits contains 14 cards. Each suit contains cards numbered through one to 10 and 4 face cards. Now, let's look at the meanings of the numbered cards in Minor Arcana.

Number 1

The number one or an ace in the tarot is the indication of something new. If there are aces in your reading, it means something new with immense potential is awaiting you in life. This represents pure energy that has no shape or home right now. Instead, this energy can be easily molded and brought to life, depending on your needs and requirements. It brings with it immense opportunities on which you can capitalize. Since the energy is raw, it is also unstable. If you don't take charge of it immediately, it will quickly overwhelm you.

Number 2

It represents pairs. It is all about unions and all the complexities involved in them. If one is about individuality, two is about pairs. According to tarot readings, number two is a representation of peace and harmony. It essentially means two opposite are coming together for the sake of creation. The balance put forth by this number might feel quite perfect. It brings with it a sense of comfort. These two factors put together can make it difficult to move forward. It can also result in difficulty when it is time to make decisions.

Number 3

Everything about group dynamics is depicted by the number 3. When a group comes together, there are different outcomes possible. Groups don't necessarily refer to individuals; they can also be ideas, opportunities or thoughts. It is also a symbolic representation of completion. In some tarot readings, it is believed that the number 3 suggests completion of the first phase.

Number 4

This number suggests there's a foundation laid down, and it is time to build on it. The primary message this number conveys is that it is time to grow and evolve in life. Unless you build and develop on the foundation, your efforts will lead to no fruition. Perhaps there were some disappointments along the way, or maybe things didn't go as planned. Regardless of the reason, number 4 in the Tarot is the universe's way of pushing you forward.

Number 5

Fives in tarot suggest change, conflict and fluctuations in life. Fives magnify the energy given out by fours. This energy encourages you to look within yourself to find the different reasons progress is important for you. So, it becomes easier to move forward despite any instability that comes your way.

Number 6

The previous number represented conflicts, while this number gives the momentum required to move away from the conflict and reach a solution. Whether or not the conflict is an internal or external one, number 6 helps find a solution. This is a card that symbolizes light after darkness.

Number 7

This number represents self-introspection and self-reflection. If sevens show up in your tarot reading, it means it's time to step back and reflect upon whatever is happening in your life. It helps reevaluate whether or not you are on the right path by assessing what you need and where you are headed. It helps you get in touch with your authentic self.

Number 8

Previously, it was mentioned that number 3 is a representation of the completion of the first phase. Number 8 is the representation of the completion of the second phase. It usually coincides with some form of achievement, whether emotional, spiritual or physical. It is an indication of growth, and it often comes in the forms we least expect.

Number 9

If number 9 shows up in your tarot reading, it means you are quite close to completion. If you are working hard on a goal, number nine suggests you are quite close to achieving it. It may also be a representation you have reached or hit a plateau and life. Even though the finishing line is near, it feels as if you have made no progress. This is the pause that comes right before a cycle and.

Number 10

Number 10 is the representation of completion of the third and final phase. This is when all your goals come to fruition. It indicates you have completed a circle, and it's time to begin again.

In tarot, the cards matter more than the numbers with which they are associated. However, numbers are helpful if you want to better understand what the cards represent. Associating numbers with the Minor Arcana is straightforward. Each number has a specific story to tell, and they play out in different ways depending on the suit they belong to.

Combining the information about individual numbers and the different suits makes it easy to understand what the tarot cards mean. For instance, let's consider the Five of Cups. Five represents love, and cups are associated with relationships. If you draw the five of cups, the tarot reading is telling you something about your love and relationships. Similarly, the five of pentacles suggests a change in association with your finances and material possessions.

Besides all the numbered cards in the Minor Arcana, there are 16 face cards of the tarot, which are known as court cards. There are four face cards present in each of the four suits in Minor Arcana. The face cards are the Page, Knight, King and the Queen. Each of these face cards shows specific energy given by the suit in the hands of different people. A simple analogy is to think of these cards as representing different stages of life. For instance, the pages are curious like children while the knights are teens or young adults, The Kings are highly skilled and grown adults while the Queens represent older and wiser figures with a deeper understanding of life. These stages can also be the journey an individual goes through in life. Everything starts with a self-development goal, an early stage, a midpoint and the end.

By understanding what the numbers mean, the representation of energy given out by different suits, and the meaning of the face cards, you can get an effective reading of an individual from their Minor Arcana cards.

The Connection Between Tarot and Numerology

There is a fascinating relationship between Major Arcana cards and the numerological life path numbers. To calculate your life part number, you need to reduce the number of your full birth date into a single digit. For instance, if an individual was born on 12.02.2001, the life path number will be 8. In the Major Arcana cards, the Birth Card is like the Life Path Number. The eight Major Arcana cards are Justice. The traits embodied by this card will correspond with the traits associated with number 8 in numerology and the Justice card in tarot. By using a combination of this, you can obtain a wealth of information about an individual's strengths and challenges. It can also be used to obtain insight into what the future holds in store for him on personal and professional fronts.

Numerology might not encompass everything tarot includes, but it can be used as a guiding tool. Tarot reading and numerological analysis go hand in hand.

Conclusion

By learning about numerology, you will finally understand the intricate relationship between science and spirituality. It proves the existence of tangibility and logic, and metaphysics. People often ask these questions on the path to self-discovery. This will act as a guide that helps you to put together the puzzle of your life. Since their discovery thousands of years ago, these concepts have been proven repeatedly. Numbers come with their own set of energy. These energies tend to influence our lives directly and indirectly.

You probably might have felt quite overwhelmed when you looked at the numerology chart for the first time. By now, you will have realized it is not that complicated. Its elegance lies in its simplicity. You don't have to be gifted to interpret numbers and understand their influence on you. As long as you are willing to learn, discovering the secrets of numerology is easy. In this book, you were given all the information you need to get started with the basics. It breaks down numerology and the easy-to-understand concepts. By calculating the influences of numbers in your life, it helps you understand your life's purpose. It might not necessarily change the course of your life, but it certainly helps you discover who you are. Self-discovery is essential for growth, and this is where numerology steps into the picture.

This is not a new concept, but its influence can still be felt in our lives. From calculating your life path number to your relationship number, there is a lot to discover. This is the perfect tool for self-discovery. While you work on calculating these numbers and understanding the true meaning and energies they give out, try to draw similarities you notice in your life and numerology teachings.

Now, all that's left for you to do is start charting the course of your life based on numerology. From calculating your birth date and numbers and understanding the influence of your name to calculating your life path and destiny numbers, you can discover a lot about yourself. This book will help you every step of the way. Commitment, curiosity and a willingness to learn are the only three things you need while discovering the world of numerology.

Once you are armed with these new insights, the next step is to leverage the power of numerology to create a life you desire. By embracing its power and making changes when required, you can finally connect with your true self. These refreshing and, at times, surprising discoveries will truly change your perception of yourself and life in general. So, what are you waiting for? Get started immediately!

Part 2: Tarot

Unlock the Power of Tarot Spreads and Learn About Psychic Tarot Card Reading, Symbolism, and Developing Your Intuition

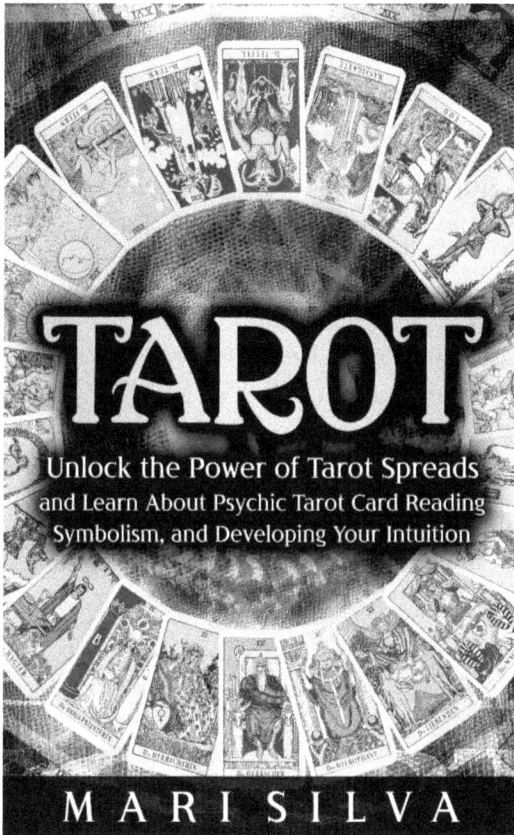

Introduction

Did you ever stop and think what it would be like if you could interpret every message the Universe has for you? Have you ever wondered if you could see into your future? If you have, then you are in the right place. Most people struggle to learn more about themselves. They may want to learn about their past, present, or future to gain a better understanding of why life is full of the various challenges that we all face. Some also want to learn more about the dangers they may encounter to prevent them. They may also want to see what happened in their past that made them behave the way they do now.

This book will help you understand yourself better. You can finally map your thoughts and emotions back to an event or situation in your life. Few people believe that a simple set of cards can do this, but do you? Even if you don't, I'm positive you will after reading this book. Whether you are a beginner or just want to refresh your memory, this is the perfect book for you.

A lot goes into tarot cards and tarot reading. This book explains the basics, and it will help you learn more about yourself through Tarot reading. The Universe has a message for everybody. You need only to be strong enough to listen to the message and interpret it. Many people have used Tarot cards to understand these messages. If you are curious to learn more about Tarot cards and their meanings, you are in the right place. This book helps you with a program paced and easy to understand.

This book looks at the basics of Tarot and introduces layouts and other important information you need if you wish to read the cards. The first chapter covers information about how you should select the right deck and the different spreads you can use. The latter chapters of the book cover the different cards found in the deck of cards. The book also covers tips and information to read tarot cards. You must adhere to these instructions so your reading is accurate. The different cards found in the Tarot deck and their interpretation has also been in the book. You can predict the future or identify a person's past using these interpretations.

There are different layouts used for a tarot reading. The three layouts most commonly used have been described. The different positions in the layout are also explained to help you identify a person's past, present, or future. To better show you how a reading works, the book also includes a sample reading to help you determine the steps you need to follow. You also learn more about the different types of cards found in a Tarot deck. We will also focus on specific cards from the Minor and Major Arcana since those are extremely important for you during a reading.

Chapter One: How to Read the Cards

Most people are wary about receiving any messages from the Universe. There are important signs and messages that the Universe leaves for you, so you must be open to receiving these messages. You can use Tarot cards to help you decipher this meaning. Each card in the deck has a different meaning because of the cards' images and the connections between them.

The Root of the Meaning

Experts believe that the meaning behind Tarot cards come from within us. Your subconscious mind helps you decipher the meaning of every card since your subconscious mind understands various aspects of your life and hence is known as your inner guide. Most people ignore their subconscious mind because they fear what the future may hold for you—the subconscious guides you to reach for any card in the deck. Since most people only rely on their conscious mind, they ignore the subconscious mind and its signals. It is only when you let your mind lead you that you find meaning when you use tarot cards.

Tarot Card Instructions

This section leaves you with instructions and tips to use when you read cards. Your understanding of tarot cards will improve when you use them. As they say, "Practice makes perfect." The instructions in this chapter and other information in the book will help you improve. Before you begin reading, you must know what the objective of your tarot reading is.

1. Before you begin the Tarot reading, before you begin to understand how to read the cards, you have to familiarize yourself with the cards. Look at the images and see if you can find any connection. Try reading on yourself before you conduct a reading for another person.

2. Study what each means and also how they can be interpreted. It is easier if you can put a meaning to the cards in the deck. It is better to know the meaning of each before you conduct a tarot reading.

Selecting the Deck

The most important thing to consider with Tarot reading is the deck. If you do not have the right deck with you, then your reading will not have the correct outcome. Every Tarot card has its own energy and meaning, so you need to make sure you choose the right deck, especially the one you connect with.

Choose a Deck You Connect With

This is the most important thing to remember. You must always choose a card you intuitively and personally connect with. You may have people around you who talk about the Rider-Waite deck, the Wild Unknown deck, or any other deck. This does not mean you should choose a deck only because someone told you about them. You can always try different decks and see which one works best for you. There may be decks that cause you to break into a sweat. This means the deck is not right for you.

If you are in love with a specific deck, use that first. If you live close to a bookstore or new age store, go to the Tarot section and pick up a deck. Play around with them. See what energy you feel when you choose a deck. Do you feel a connection, either intuitive or personal, when you hold the deck in your hand? If you want to purchase a deck online, you can always look for them on Google. Go through the images in every deck and see if a connection. Always stick to your intuition.

Understand the Imagery

Look at the cards in every deck you choose and go through every one of them. If you are looking at the deck online, look at as many images as you can on any social media platform. You can use the hashtag #fountaintarot to look for them on social media. There are numerous hashtags you can use for the same.

When you look at the images, analyze how you react to the image on the card. Do you like the patterns and colors? Do you find other decks or images more attractive? For instance, someone may prefer the Fairy deck because of the bright colors and images. Others prefer the Radiant Rider-Waite deck because of the bright colors used in the images.

Also, look at every card and get a sense of what each means to you. You must look at both the Minor and Major Arcana cards. Some decks do not have a story or imagery on the Minor Arcana cards. This does not help you choose the right deck online since you cannot view all the cards in the deck. If you choose such a deck, you should go to the store and buy them.

Know Your Level

Most beginners prefer to use popular Tarot decks since they are easy to understand. One such example is the Rider-Waite deck. This deck's imagery is easy to understand. The images are practical and straightforward. Since this is a popular deck, there is a lot of information available on the Internet to help you understand how to use the deck better. You can also choose a deck with minimalist and clear imagery to help you connect better with the symbols. If you are an experienced reader or want to look at a complex deck, choose a different tarot deck. One such example is the Thoth Tarot deck. This deck of cards is known for its depth and complexity. You can also use other abstract decks.

You need not limit yourself to a simple or popular deck if you are new to Tarot. You can always choose the deck you connect with, both personally and intuitively.

Modern or Traditional?

Have you always thought of using traditional or old Tarot decks? If yes, you can choose different decks, such as the Original Rider Waite Tarot deck, Visconti Tarot deck, or Tarot de Marseilles deck. If you are drawn to more modern Tarot decks, pick whichever one feels right for you. The new Tarot decks that are coming now are brilliant. The imagery relates to the current times and has beautiful artwork. Did you know you could also create your very own deck using different imagery and artwork? You can have a knight roaming the streets or even have a beautiful cup designed for the deck.

Read "The Little White Book"

Tarot decks often come with their own books that explain the imagery and artwork used on the cards. Some decks come with more information when compared to other decks. Some decks have minimal or no information. To know what every card in the Tarot deck means, you must read the Little White Book that comes with every Tarot deck. This book will usually give you all the information you need about the different cards in the deck. If the book that comes with the deck does not have enough information, you can always check if there is any information about that deck on the Internet. You can let your intuition help you determine the meaning behind every card in the deck. If you can do this, you can understand every card in the deck without a book.

Choose the Right Fit

Every Tarot deck comes in different sizes. Always choose the right size for your reading sessions. You can use tarot decks when you read at parties or for small groups. To use the deck for personal readings, you should choose a face-to-face client reading. You can also read them on the go if you use the mini tarot cards.

The size of the deck is important, especially for shuffling and handling the cards. If they are too small or big, it may become difficult for both you and the clients to handle. So, use the cards, practice with them, and learn to handle them before you perform any reading.

Determine the Objective

Always determine what the objective of your tarot readings is. You also need to know how you want to connect with them. Do you want to find love? Are you looking for peace and quiet? Choose the Tarot deck basis for your objective. The best thing about Tarot decks is that you can choose from different backgrounds. Since you have multiple options, you can choose the one that fits your desires and needs. If you are a professional, you must choose from different decks best suited for you and your situation.

Shuffling the Deck

Every reading starts here. You need to shuffle them well, but few people know how to do this. This is one of the most fundamental aspects of card reading, but they often go unmentioned. There are different tricky elements to a Tarot reading, and if you do not perform aspects of Tarot cards correctly, the reading will be incorrect. This deck is one of the most important aspects that need close attention.

This section covers techniques to help you shuffle your deck correctly, but before we look at these techniques, let us focus on why you need to shuffle these cards. If you look at it simply, you bond with them and images when you shuffle the deck. You and the cards begin to share the same energy. When you handle the cards well, you step into the same energy space as the cards. This is when you begin conversing with them.

When you shuffle cards, you give yourself enough time to focus on the topic or question. This helps you interact emotionally, physically, and spiritually with the deck. Experts recommend you use this time to begin your readings since you are shifting from the usual mindset into the world of tarot reading. This is a powerful and simple ritual that will help you do the same.

Now, let us look at the different techniques. Understand that there is no right or wrong way to shuffle the tarot deck. You can shuffle them in any way you want. Each tarot reader has his/her own way to shuffle the cards, and you may come across different methods. If you go to a Tarot reading event, you will come across different styles. Some may pile them, while others may rearrange the cards gently. You may come across some readers who bang the cards to shuffle them.

You can work with the approaches mentioned in this section and invent a style for yourself. When you begin Tarot reading, you will know which method works best for you. Do not worry if you feel awkward when you read Tarot cards. Since the cards in a Tarot deck are larger than a regular deck of cards, it takes time for one to handle them with ease.

Some suggest that you are disrespecting them if you do not handle them well, but this is not true since we all forge a different relationship with the cards in our decks. If you perform a tarot reading with bad intentions, you are disrespectful. If you approach Tarot reading with a good attitude, it does not matter if you drop them on the floor. Let us now learn how you can shuffle Tarot cards.

4 Ways to Shuffle Tarot Cards

The Classic Shuffle

This is the simplest shuffle. You need only to divide the deck into two piles and shift the piles to make sure the cards interweave. You can use a bridge shuffle to try a fancy shuffle. You may take time to get the hang of this when you use tarot cards, but this is one of the easiest and fastest ways to shuffle the deck.

Regrouping and Spreading

This is an evocative method. Spread them on the table, so it looks good to you. You can stick to a pattern based on aesthetics. So, get fancy with the spread. When you regroup the cards, try using a different pattern to pick them up.

Pile the Cards

Divide them into smaller piles. Group them in a different order. You can either shuffle the pairs and then pile them together or shuffle the deck when it is integrated.

Shuffle in Your Hands

This is a very simple method. You split the deck of cards in your hand and place them in different stops in the deck. This may be difficult to do when you start tarot reading. The process but is a great way to get in the zone. This is a meditative and comforting technique to handle all the cards in the deck before you read them.

Tarot Card Spreads

Most people do not know how to choose the spread that works for them. There are many spreads to choose from, and you can work with them all before choosing the one that works for you. This section covers simple tarot card spreads you can use when you start off with tarot card reading. There are other spreads you can use, but those are often complicated to use. The spreads covered in this section can be used by a beginner easily.

The three-card spread is one of the most commonly used spreads, and this is one that most beginners use for their first reading. The other common spread is the five-card and Celtic cross spread. You can choose any of these spreads, depending on your convenience. These spreads help you answer all your questions. Some spreads may use only one card from the deck, while others may use the entire deck.

Every spread has its characteristics and attributes, and these give the spreads their power. Some Tarot spreads are standardized, while tarot readers can develop other spreads. You can develop your own Tarot spread depending on your style and requirement. You can base these layouts on certain adjustments you may want to make to the layout. This section does not cover every spread but covers the most important and common ones.

There are many spreads used for a tarot reading. Of those, the three-card spread, five-card spread, and Celtic-cross spread are the most famous.

The Three-Card Spread

The three-card spread is the easiest spread for a Tarot reading, especially if you are a beginner. You can use this spread to gain an insight into the present, past, and future. You cannot use a Tarot reading to predict what may happen in the future, but reading can help you determine what or how you may feel in the future. First, work on the three-card spread before you work on the other two spreads mentioned in this section.

Draw three cards from the deck and spread them in the following manner:

⬜⬜⬜

The card in the center will tell you about yourself or the person you are performing the reading for. The card will tell you how you are feeling about yourself. You can use the card on the left to learn more about the different obstacles and opportunities that come your way, while the one on your right helps you determine the solution.

Celtic Cross Spread

This is one of the most popular spreads used by both beginners and experts. The layout is straightforward, but it holds great energy and power. Since there is strong energy around this spread, people have used it to answer numerous questions. Many secret societies also use this spread to answer different questions about their life.

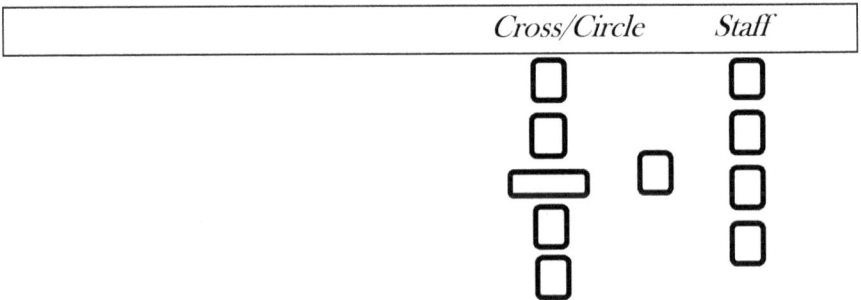

Cross/Circle   Staff

There are two parts to the Celtic cross – the circle or cross and the staff. The former has six cards, while the latter has four cards. The circle or cross resembles the Celtic cross found in Ireland. The cross in Ireland has many spokes placed perpendicular to each other. These spokes are linked using a circle. This symbol is a connection between the matter of all events and beings at a certain time and the spirit. It is believed that the energy within the spokes is feminine and works with the masculine energy present in the staff. The Celtic cross spread is a representation of the duality of nature. This spread and energy represent the polarity of the human psyche.

The circle or cross-section of the spread has two crosses. The smaller cross is at the center of the spread. There are two cards that make the cross in the center. The bigger cross has six cards, including the small cross in the center. The larger cross helps you identify and understand various events that have occurred in the past and those that may occur in the future. The card on the left of the cross depicts the past, while the one on the right depicts the future. The cards at the top and bottom of the cross depict the conscious and subconscious minds, respectively.

The cards in the Staff section of the spread describe your life. These rarely relate to the present. You need to let your intuition guide you in interpreting the spread. You can understand your future better and also help people understand their future better.

Five-Card Spread

The three-card spread helps you obtain a lot of information, but the five-card spread helps you dive into the question's details. You can use either the three-card or five-card spread to find the root cause of any problem. You can spread the five-card spread in the form of a cross. It is often structured in this way. The base of the five-card spread is the three-card spread. In this spread, three cards will relate to the past, present, and future in the center of the cross.

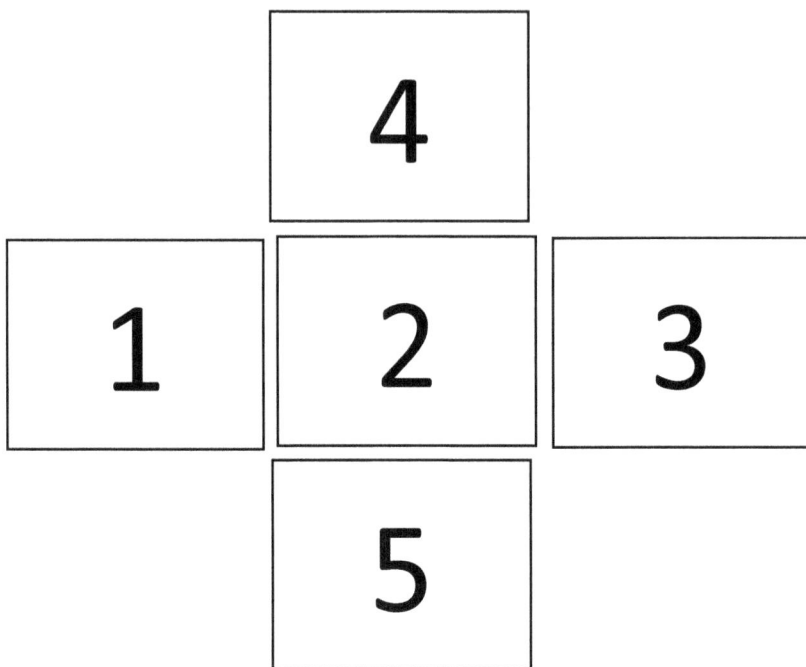

1. Past

2. Present

3. Future

4. Core reason for circumstances

5. Potential of situation

The cards may not represent the actual outcome, but they will show you the brightest and darkest situations and outcomes hidden in the current situation.

You can also use a rectangular formation when you use the five-card spread. You can use this formation to explore various situations and themes. The spread makes it easy to look at different variations. When you use the rectangular formation, the theme or the main card is placed between the other four cards. You need to pull the theme card last.

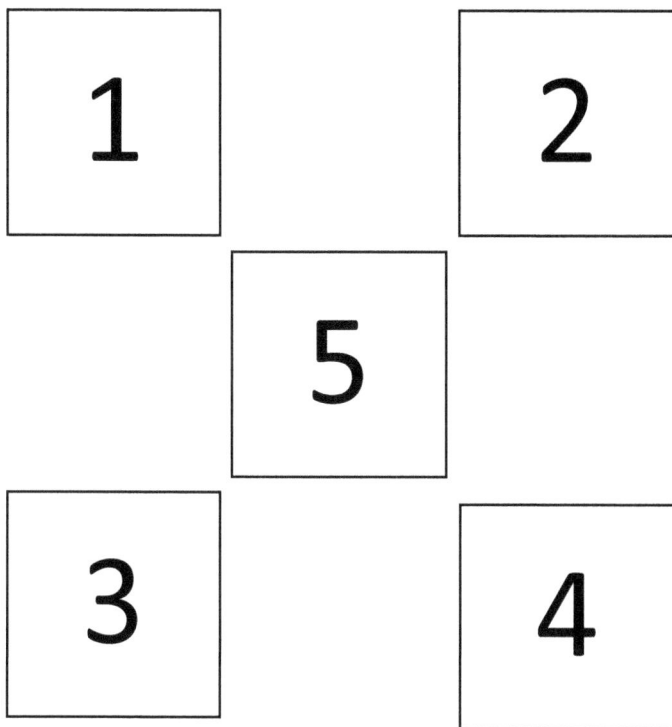

1   2

5

3   4

1. Present situation

2. Influences

3. Challenges

4. Final outcome

5. Theme

Some readers prefer using the other four cards in the formation to understand the theme. They make loose interpretations of these cards when they pull them out of the deck, but you can choose what each position should represent. For example, these cards can represent your conflicts, fears, desires, and another's perspective or any lesson you may need to learn.

How to Interpret Reversed Cards

When you obtain a reversed card in your reading, it can be interpreted in different ways. It is for this reason a reversed card is extremely important to read carefully. A reversed card can be interpreted in multidimensional ways. Only when you do this can you understand or answer any questions you may have about your life. A reversed card holds as much importance as an upright card in a tarot reading, and you can make the right decisions based on the reading of these cards. You need to consider these components of reversed cards before you read or interpret them:

1. Understand the meaning and interpretation of a reversed card. The later chapters in the book talk about how to interpret the different cards in the tarot deck.

2. Understand how you should interpret the card when it is in the upright position

3. Look for ways to determine the increase and decrease in energy levels of the card

4. Learn to combine the meaning of upright and reversed cards during a reading

5. Is there any energy blocked or repressed in the reversed card?

It is easier to use your previous experience to determine how you should interpret the card.

Chapter Two: Developing Intuition

Have you ever gone to a reading where the person reading the cards for you does not know what to say? You wonder if they have forgotten what the card means. This frustrates you because you went there to understand something about yourself, and the lack of information frustrates you. This can happen to you, as well. Here is where you may want to open the Little White Book and read everything about the card, including its meaning. Does this help you, though? Will your reading help the person?

Sure, you can use your book to help you understand the cards, but are you sure the meaning and symbolism are accurate? This need not be the case. You may feel doubt on numerous occasions if you do not develop your intuition. You may feel one thing when you look at the card, but the book you are using will tell you something else.

What should you do here? How will you correctly identify the meaning of the tarot card? Never ignore your intuition since this is the key to understanding every card's meaning in the deck you use. Interpret the meaning of the cards in the deck with confidence and ease. This chapter will look at how to understand the meaning of a tarot card using your intuition. We will also look at steps you can use to improve your intuition. Intuitive tarot reading is the best way to perform a reading since you are not trying to force the card's meaning from the white book into your reading. The book's meaning can have a different meaning, and you may interpret the imagery and symbolism differently.

Developing Intuition

One of the best ways to develop your intuition is through meditation. Through meditation, you can delve deeper into the symbolism and meaning every tarot card offers. You can go around your conscious mind and focus on the message the card has for you. This helps you connect with your intuition. When you learn to relax your mind, you learn to control your thought process. You open up the path towards your subconscious mind, making it easier for you to tap into your intuition. You learn to let your intuition tell you what to make of the tarot card in front of you. In this process, you need to relax your body and mind. This is the only way you can understand the imagery and symbolism of the Tarot card you have chosen.

Choose the Card

When you use this technique, you learn more about the tarot card. This helps you improve your intuition. Shuffle the deck and choose any card from the deck. If you have a specific card in mind, place it in front of you. You can use a card based on a specific situation or event in your life. For instance, to invite love into life, select the Lovers card. You can also choose the Two Cups card.

Set the Ambiance

You need to choose the place and time when you want to work on developing your intuition. Choose a spot and time when you know you will not be disturbed. Be comfortable and disconnect from the world. Get rid of any distractions. If you want it to be completely quiet, you can wear earbuds. Alternatively, you can listen to a meditation CD if it helps you concentrate. You can also dim the lights and burn incense sticks. Sit straight because lying down will only make you sleepy. Place the tarot card you have selected before you.

Focus on Your Breath

When you find yourself in a comfortable position, focus on your breath. Breathe normally and only through your nose. When you breathe in, observe what you feel when you breathe in. How do you feel when the air passes through your nostrils? Continue to breathe normally and focus on the sensation of the air on your breath. If you find thoughts flitting through your mind, observe them, and then let go of them. Think of them as clouds floating away. When you manage to do this, you should go back to focusing on your breath.

Relax

Now, focus on your body. Take a deep breath and let the air enter your body. Feel every molecule in the air you have breathed in; fill every inch of your body with energy. When you breathe out, imagine every muscle and cell in your body relaxing. Move your focus to your head, eyes, shoulders, neck, arms, chest, back, hips, legs, and toes. Let your body relax. When you feel like you are floating, you will be at peace.

Focus on the Card

Place the tarot card you have selected in front of you and focus on it. Do not glare at the card but look at it with a soft gaze. Take two or three deep breaths. If you find thoughts entering your mind, do not give them any importance. You should observe them and think of them floating away like clouds. Focus on your breath and look at the tarot card in front of you.

Now focus on the card and imagine that the figures are growing larger in front of you. Imagine that the figures and images are becoming life-size. Now, imagine yourself stepping into the imagery in the card. Look at your surroundings and observe what you see. Ask yourself who is with you on the card. Make a note of the colors and objects that stand out.

Walk towards an object you connect within the card and touch it. Feel the texture and observe what you feel and hear. Smell the air around you. If you find something you can eat, walk towards that object and taste it. Once you have done this, imagine you are a figure in the card. Become this person on the card. How do you feel about being this figure? How do you think or feel when you are this person? What is your attitude towards your circumstances as this person? Now talk to yourself in the same way you think the character would talk to you. What do you want to tell yourself? What message or advice do you want to give?

Look at your surroundings one more time. Is there something that makes you happy? Does one specific area or object in the surroundings give you energy? Does anything in the imagery concern you? Are you anxious about something in the imagery? Can you notice the areas in your body that feel the tension and anxiety? Is it possible for you to release that nervous energy?

Look at the various symbols and objects on the card. How can you use them? Is there a symbolic meaning for the objects you have picked up? Why do you think the objects and symbols are around you? Pay attention to your surroundings one last time and note what you did not find the last time you looked at the imagery. You are almost done, so step out of the figure in the card. Now, slowly step out of the card. Focus on the card until it reaches its size.

Awaken

You must acknowledge all the work you have completed until the moment. You should also know that you could always go back to your zone of peace and quiet whenever you want. Slowly bring your focus to your surroundings. Take a few deep breaths and feel the surrounding energy fill your feet, belly, hands, and your entire body. If you have closed your eyes, slowly open them. You will feel energized and refreshed.

Understand and Note Your Insights

When you are done with your meditation process, make a note of everything you saw. Also, write down your thoughts and emotions. Keep a separate journal to write these down.

Chapter Three: The Major Arcana

These cards are the most important cards in the deck. These cards represent various karmic influences, archetypal themes, and life lessons. These cards talk about those experiences that influence your journey. The cards in this Arcana are complex and deep in many ways. These cards are synonymous with human consciousness and tell you the stories and lessons passed through the years.

The Major Arcana includes 22 cards – one unnumbered and 21 numbered cards. These cards are called the Trump cards. The unnumbered card, known as The Fool, is an important part of the Major Arcana. The character is very important since he meets new teachers and learns various lessons on his journey. When he reaches the World card, he finally completes his journey. This journey is called the Fool's journey and is one of the best ways to understand Major Arcana's cards.

What Does a Card From this Arcana Mean?

When you look at a card from the Major Arcana during a Tarot reading session, you are being asked to reflect on various themes and lessons you are experiencing. The cards in this Arcana set the scene for the entire session since every other card you pick from the deck will relate to the Major arcana card.

Is it Okay to Have a Majority of Major Arcana Cards During a Reading?

If you pull out too many cards from the major arcana during a reading, it implies that you are going through some life-changing events, and these events will have a long-term effect. The cards indicate that you should pay attention to what is happening in your life so you can proceed further in your personal and spiritual quest. If any of the Arcana cards are reversed, it indicates you are not focusing on those aspects of your life, so first focus on them before you move forward.

There are 22 cards that fall under the major arcana. This section lists the names of these cards and how they can be interpreted for a reading.

- The Cards
- The Fool

This card shows you are spontaneous. It indicates that you face the world with your head held high, but you do not consider the problems and issues you may encounter in the process.

The Magician

The magician is an active card depicting your conscious awareness. This card states you are charismatic and have the willpower to take over any challenge that life throws at you.

High Priestess

The high priestess depicts your mysterious subconscious. This card indicates you have an inherent potential you have not realized. When you realize this potential, you can achieve whatever you want.

The Empress

This card indicates to you that you are attracted to an individual. It represents the natural and sensual aspects of the world. It is also called Juno, who is the Queen of all Roman gods. This card also represents feminine characteristics.

The Emperor

This card depicts the Father. It shows you are subjected to multiple rules in life. It also indicates that you do great under these conditions and finds a way to meet your goals and dreams.

The Hierophant

This card indicates you will meet with a spiritual advisor or mentor. You will connect with them and also grow on your spiritual journey.

The Lovers

This card can be interpreted as you being ready to enter a relationship. But this does not necessarily mean it will be a healthy relationship. You might have to work on the relationship to make it last.

The Chariot

The Chariot depicts your will power. It shows you have the power to achieve greatness and victory in your life.

Strength, Judgment, and Temperance

These cards indicate exactly what their name suggests. You will know how strong you are and also more about your morals.

Hermit

This card depicts that you are in search of knowledge, which could mean anything.

Wheel of Fortune

This card indicates that you will experience a change in life. Based on the different influences in your life, you can predict the changes you will have.

Hanged Man

This card shows you are a person who has sacrificed a lot in life. It also indicates this will continue.

Death

This card does not mean you are nearing death. It only implies there are certain habits or aspects of your personality you may have to change. It just means you will be moving on from a certain path of living into another.

Devil

This card will help you understand the different external factors affecting you, but you are ignorant of these external factors, so it is difficult for you to overcome your problems.

Tower

The card tells you that you will discover something new about yourself soon.

Star, Moon, and Sun

These cards talk about the effect of the astronomical bodies on your life. They depict the softness, calmness, and brightness of the sun, moon, and stars.

World

This card talks about your happiness. It tells you about whether you are happy with yourself and the surrounding environment. It helps you understand what you feel most content with.

Chapter Four: The Fool's Journey

Upright

Key Meaning or Interpretation

Freedom, new beginnings, travel, adventure, innocence, originality, carelessness, foolishness, travel, youth, idealism, lack of commitment, spontaneity

General Interpretation

This is the first card of the Major Arcana, and as mentioned above, it indicates new beginnings. If you pull this card during your reading, it means you may experience a new adventure soon. The adventure will take you on a path where you need to take a leap of faith. You will but learn from the experience and grow as an individual. Here, the new adventure can be anything – it can even mean you may move to a new country. You will welcome the change this card indicates to you. The Fool has a positive meaning, but it will take you a while to interpret the card's correct meaning when the card appears with other cards.

Romance

This card is both spontaneous and exciting, but it is a little ambiguous. If you are in a relationship, this card indicates that you are very excited about being in love and cannot contain your emotions. If another person is asking you whether they can be in a committed relationship, this card means the person is not ready to commit to a relationship. If you are single, this card can mean you will enter into a carefree and impulsive romance. If the card appears, be prepared for a beautiful and fun relationship. You should keep your eyes open so you do not miss true love.

Profession

If you have pulled this card out, it means the opportunity will come knocking on your door. You can take a leap of faith and start your business or start a new job. There may be people around you who do not know what you are doing or put you down but learn to be patient with them. Explain to them what you want to do, but do not let their words deter you. If you are working on projects at the moment, the card indicates that you will work on the project with renewed energy and fresh ideas. This card indicates there will be advancements in the project. Do your research and be extremely clever. Do not be afraid. Work hard on any new move or project.

Health

This card is a great indicator of physical health. If you are ill, the card indicates that you will regain your energy and strength. The card also indicates that you are prone to meeting with an accident, so you need to be extra careful. The card can also bring good news since it indicates pregnancy or the start of a new life.

Spirituality

This card indicates you are at the start of your new journey. You will learn more about your journey and see how you will move onto a new path. Since the card indicates renewed energy, you will be eager to try numerous approaches. There will be people who cannot understand your journey but always do what is best for you.

Reversed

Carelessness, recklessness, stupidity, apathy, irrationality, distraction, negligence, lack of hope, faith, or fun

General Interpretation

The meaning of the reversed card is the same as the upright card, a new beginning. When you reverse this card, it indicates that the new beginning may not be one you are keen to consider. The new beginning is coming your way. The reversed card indicates that you are behaving recklessly towards the people around you. The card can imply a lack of fun, hope, faith, and irrational thinking.

Romance

When reversed, this card indicates that your pursuit of adventure will hold you back from the love you want or need. It can also cause uncertainty and problems in any relationship. If this card is reversed, it could mean that your relationship may involve some excitement. This card implies that new issues and problems may crop up in your relationship.

Profession

When this card is reversed, it shows financial opportunities that can be promising. You need to exercise caution. You must do your homework before you ever commit to something new. You should never let the people around you take advantage of you. You may become restless in your position at work and probably want to start your own business. Think before you do anything. You should never let yourself be held back because of a lack of confidence. Never be afraid and know that your ideas are valid.

Health

When this card is reversed, it means you can try different means to resolve any issues you may have. If you have the reversed card in your reading, it means you are accident-prone, and you must know your surroundings.

Spiritual

When you look at the card in a spiritual context, the reversed card indicates that you are looking for a new experience. You want to get rid of your old habits and patterns. You may surprise people around you but do what pleases you.

Understanding the Fool's Journey

As mentioned earlier, the Fool's journey is only a metaphor. This card's journey is an indicator of your journey and the different phases you go through in life. The cards in the Major Arcana indicates the journey that the Fool will go through. Here are the steps that the Fool will go through in life:

- The Fool learns all his life lessons from the other cards in the Arcana.

- This card represents those people taking on a new adventure. It can also talk about people leaving home for the first time.

- The card also represents those graduating, moving to a new city, starting a new company or job, and others.

- The card represents those individuals who are excited and brave to take up anything that comes their way.

- This card indicates that the individual is on the path to finding oneself. It also indicates that the person is keen to incorporate all his learnings to overcome different situations.

As mentioned earlier, there are 22 cards in the major arcana. Each card represents an important life lesson that the Fool will learn. The Major Arcana cards represent experiences that every individual will go through at some point in his life. The next two chapters talk about the 22 cards in the Major Arcana and how they relate to an individual's experience.

Chapter Five: Major Cards 1 – 11

The Magician

Upright Position

Key Meanings

Influence, power, resourcefulness, willpower, ability, skill, intellect, psychic powers, logic, and concentration

General Interpretation

When this card appears in your reading, it means you have all the abilities and skills you need to succeed. The Universe will do whatever it can to align all the positive changes your way. This card shows you should use your concentration, willpower, and intellect to ensure what happens. When you pull this card out during your reading, it means you have the ability and power to achieve your goals. The card also refers to the people in your life who can help you achieve your goals. You can contact the people around you from whom you can learn.

Romance

This card indicates a positive outcome in your life. If you are in a relationship, this card means you will move to a deeper and new level in your relationship where you will commit to each other. If you are single, the card indicates that now is the best time for you to meet somebody. Your partner will always be serious about you and will treat you well.

Profession

With Profession, this card indicates that you will have new opportunities. This means you will need to be brave and use your original ideas to improve your skills. Do not tell people your ideas because it does not bode well to give away your secrets. The card indicates that you will be promoted. You will feel self-assured and powerful. You should remember that great things would come your way. This card signifies that you will be presented with new tasks and opportunities. You may get the chance to mentor someone or may even mentor someone else. The card indicates that your finances will improve soon, and you will make money due to new opportunities.

Health

Your good health and strength will come back if you feel drained or have been ill recently. If your health no longer improves, you may need to try new alternative therapies. This card indicates that you need to approach a powerful and experienced healer so you have the boost you need.

Spirituality

In terms of spirituality, this card indicates now is a great time for you to work on spiritual development. If you have always had an interest in the subject of spirituality, you can now concentrate on this area. This will help you manage spirituality and channel your magical energy easily. You will be surprised to see how you will benefit from this new learning if you learn to concentrate and channel your energy. If you are interested in psychic development, this card indicates that you have latent abilities.

Reversed Position

Key Meaning or Interpretation

Greed, manipulation, trickery, untrustworthiness, conniving, unused ability, lack of mental clarity, and cunning

General Interpretation

When the reverse of this card appears in your reading, it indicates that you need to be careful about any opportunities. You should never let your doubt stop you from choosing or working on an opportunity. If the card refers to any person, it means this person is trying to manipulate or use you despite them being trustworthy and knowledgeable. Look out for greedy and deceitful people and always be careful about the people you trust.

Romance

If you are in a relationship, and this card has appeared in your life, it means you need to be more honest and open with your partner. To manipulate a situation to ensure you get whatever you want, you should never do that. It is best to use honesty to fulfill your needs and desires. This card also indicates that your partner may be selfish and mean, despite him or her appearing to be trustworthy. If you are single, this card suggests that you are becoming very cynical about your future life. You may feel like you will not attract the right people in your life. You should never lose faith. Remember to stay positive and always send light and love into the world.

Money and Career

If the reverse card appears in your reading, it indicates that you are not using your skills and abilities to the fullest. You must learn to make the best use of all the opportunities available to you. If you are experiencing self-doubt, find a way to overcome it and achieve your goals. Spend time to understand why you feel the way you do and determine what is holding you back. This card indicates that the people around you often hold you back from taking on a new adventure. If you find yourself stuck in a rut because of your finances, take the right approach and change your circumstances.

Health

This card is a positive card when it comes to health, regardless of whether it is in the upright or reversed position. It indicates that you should trust in your ability to heal, so you can kick start the process of healing. If you do suffer from any mental health issues, meet with a professional soon.

Spirituality

This card indicates that you should no longer follow your old spiritual path. It is important for you to explore a new path and remove the old beliefs you may have had about your spirituality. Try to get rid of any beliefs that hinder your ability to function or work. You can use different methods to discover your spirituality. God also indicates that you must only use your power and prowess for good.

The High Priestess

Upright Position

Key Meanings

Unattainability, desirability, mystery, spirituality, creativity, subconscious, thirst for knowledge, sensuality, fertility, higher power

General Interpretation

The card represents these characteristics:

- Common sense
- Intuition
- Sensuality

- Mystery

If this card appears in your reading, it indicates that you should now trust your gut feeling and behave in accordance with those feelings. Also, pay attention to various signs, symbols, and images that the Universe is sending your way, especially when you pick this card up during your reading.

Romance

If you are a woman, this card indicates that many people around you will soon want you. If you are a man, this card indicates that you will soon find someone who will leave an impression on you. If you are in a relationship, this card indicates that you will have great sex in the next few days to come.

Profession

This card indicates that you will soon come across an opportunity that will improve your position in your job. You will receive information to help you climb the ladder with ease. This card indicates inspiration and creativity. If you are a student, the card's appearance during your reading indicates you will have a good teacher shortly. You must make sure not to discuss your finances with everybody. Give people only the information they need to know.

Health

This card indicates that you should listen to what your body has to say to you when it comes to health. You must learn to identify the signals your body leaves for you to understand what needs to be done. If this appears in your reading, it means you and the people around you are not concerned about your health. Do not let people ignore your feelings and emotions.

Spirituality

This card indicates wisdom and spirituality. If the card appears during a reading, it is time for you to connect with your intuition and inner voice. This is the only way you can trust the higher power. This card is another great indicator of your psychic abilities.

Reversed Position

Key Meanings

Lack of self-belief, unwanted attention, repression of intuition, uncontrolled sexual tension, sporadic outbursts, fertility issues, blocked psychic powers.

General Interpretation

In the upright and reversed positions, this card indicates that you should trust your intuition, and it will guide you if you listen to it. However, the card in this position indicates that you are not paying attention to your intuition. You are probably focusing more on what people around you think. You want to please them regardless of what your intuition has to say. If this card appears in your reading, it means you are not taking care of yourself. Learn to trust your intuition because you have all the knowledge and wisdom you need.

Romance

If this card appears in the reading, it means that people around you will want you, but you will question their motives. You will not like the attention they shower on you. If you are in a relationship, you may have sexual tension and emotional outbursts. You may soon lose patience and will look for a way to argue with your partner. This card indicates you need to give yourself time.

Profession

This card indicates that you are not being kept in the loop in the current project. It also indicates that the people at work do not care for your inputs. They may isolate you, and this leaves you feeling unwanted. This card also means there are duplicitous people around you, and you should maintain a close circle. Make sure to read every document placed in front of you before you sign a contract or take a loan. If it does not feel right, then do not do it.

Health

This card in the reversed position means you are lazy and need to be active. The card may also indicate menstruation issues in women and other issues, such as fertility issues and hormonal imbalances. Try different methods and treatments if the methods do not help you.

Spirituality

If this card appears in your reading, it means you are no longer in touch with your spirituality. Your intuition knows what you need to do, but you cannot grasp the message. Also, make sure you do not depend entirely on mediums or psychics to decipher these messages.

The Empress

Upright Position

Key Meanings

Fertility, pregnancy, sensuality, creativity, motherhood, femininity, art, harmony, beauty, nature

General Interpretation

This card indicates motherhood and femininity. This is one of the strongest cards in the major arcana, and if it comes in your reading, it means you will soon find fulfillment. If you are a parent, this card indicates that you should learn to communicate well with your kids. Even if you are not a kid, and this card appears in your reading, it means you should embrace the soft side of your personality. Explore your emotions and trust your intuition. People around you will be drawn to you since you are compassionate, empathetic, and calm.

Romance

This card is extremely positive, and if you are single and see it in your reading, it indicates that love will find you. If you are already in a relationship, it means you will be committed to each other and more affectionate and loving. This card also indicates good sex. If you enjoy the romance in your current relationship, remember that this card is a strong pregnancy indicator. If you are not ready to be a parent, take the necessary precautions.

Profession

If this card appears in your reading, it means you will inspire everybody around you. You will feel creative and passionate about your work. Your creativity will help you develop new ideas, and if you are looking for a change in role, this will be the best time to do it. This card indicates that your finances will be healthy, and there is a steady cash inflow, so it is the right time to invest in shares and other investment options. When you reap these investments' benefits, you should learn to share the reward with those who most need it.

Health

This card indicates pregnancy, so if you are trying to get pregnant, this card indicates success. If you do not want to get pregnant but can get pregnant, you need to exercise caution. This card also acts as a warning – if you are not looking to get pregnant and pick up this card during a reading, it means you are not nurturing yourself enough. You must take time out of your schedule to unwind and relax. This is the only way you can manage your energy levels.

Spirituality

When this card appears in your reading, it indicates that you need to focus on your intuition and listen to it. Take time to relax and listen to what your intuition is saying to you. Remember that your intuition is right, and if you have not been doing this until now, start now. When this card appears in your reading, you know you can connect with your subconscious mind or higher power. When you do this, you can connect better with the cards.

Reversed Position

Key Meanings

Lack of confidence, infertility, lack of growth, negligence, overbearing tendencies, insecurity, and disharmony

General Interpretation

If the card appears in the reverse position during a reading, it indicates you should accept your feminine qualities. It is important to remember that everybody has a mixture of feminine and masculine qualities. This card in the reversed position indicates you have neglected your feminine characteristics and qualities. This is especially true for men since they tend to ignore their feminine characteristics. Try to focus more on things that matter in life rather than the mental and material aspects of your life. This causes disharmony that will make it harder for you to think about others for a change. You may also be emotionally overwhelmed. Your confidence may also take a hit, and you may not find yourself attractive. This is when you need to focus on the ground and balance the energies within yourself.

Romance

When this card shows up in your reading, it means there are many people pursuing you, but they do not know the real you since you are afraid to show them who you are. Do not pretend to be someone else only because you want to gain the approval of the person in whom you are interested. If you are in a relationship, this card means you are not true to your partner. You are keeping your emotions at bay so you can balance the relationship. Maybe you fear rejection if you reveal your true feelings to your partner. Take time to think about what you want from the relationship and why you are suppressing your emotions. Always be mindful of your behavior since you can be overbearing. This is only because of your insecurities. The easiest way to overcome these emotions is to shift the focus back on your thoughts and emotions. Let your intuition and inner thoughts guide you to become the inspiring, beautiful, and confident person you are.

Profession

This card in this position indicates that you no longer like your work. It has become a part of your routine and is monotonous because you want to move into a creative field. You are probably not appreciated enough at work, but this need not be the case. Your emotions and thoughts make you feel this way. Do not make hasty decisions regarding your career, especially if you are not up for it yet. Spend time to understand the problem and the root of it. You may have enough money, but you do not feel confident about it. Make the right choices, so you are secure financially in the long run.

Health

The card indicates that you need to focus on your health and take care of yourself. This card in the reversed position means you will have emotional conflicts that will lead to binge eating, laziness, lethargy, and apathy, so do everything you can to make yourself feel better about yourself. If you place this card in this position during your reading, it indicates pregnancy and infertility issues.

Spirituality

When this card appears in your reading in terms of spirituality, it means you no longer connect with your intuition. This means various aspects of your life will also not function the way you need them to. It is important for you to reconnect with your intuition, so you find the link that will help you overcome any issues in your life.

The Emperor

Upright Position

Key Meanings

Stability, father figure, protectiveness, practical, authority, older man, fatherhood, dependability, practical, structure, logical

General Interpretation

If you look at the card carefully, you can see that the Emperor is an older man. The card indicates that the person is good at work and possibly wealthy. If this card appears in your reading, it means you are a grounded and powerful protector, but you can also be stubborn and rigid. Alternatively, the card can indicate to the person you are currently in a relationship with. This card indicates that the individual does not like having fun and would rather spend time on work. The Emperor's children often fall short of his expectations, and they tend to have self-esteem issues.

If you pull the card and place it in the past position, it means you had an authoritarian father figure in your life. He did have your best interests but could rarely shower you with love and affection. If the card does appear in the future or present positions, it means someone is watching out for you – a person will give you the right advice to help you improve your life.

If the card resembles nobody in your life, it can signify that you trust logic over emotion. The card signifies focus, stability, concentration, and structure you need in life to succeed.

Romance

If you are interested in men and single, the appearance of this card in your reading can mean you will find yourself romantically involved with an older man. This individual will like order, routine, logic, and structure. Since he is more stoic than romantic, he cannot show affection. He is protective, practical, and dependable. If you are single and interested in women, this card indicates you need to be more open with your emotions. If you are interested in someone, do not wait for them to approach you. Go break the ice and let them know how you feel. This card indicates monogamy; if you have had trouble in your relationship in the past, this card indicates that it will improve in the days to come.

Profession

If the Emperor card has appeared in your reading, it indicates that people will recognize your hard work and appreciate you. Perseverance, concentration, and focus are the only means to succeed in life. If you are looking for a new job, you must be persistent in your search. You need to use logic when you apply for any position. Trust that the right opportunities will come your way, and you will have structure in your career. The card can also indicate that an older team member or boss will support and guide you. With your finances, this card indicates that you need to be practical and responsible with your finances. Control your spending and always know where the money is going. This does not mean you need to control every penny that goes out of your pocket, but you need to avoid any unnecessary spending.

Health

This card indicates that you are not giving yourself enough rest. Stop performing any unnecessary activities, especially those that cause more harm to your body. You no longer have to exercise for hours but should learn to be kind to your body. If you suffer from an illness, this card's appearance in your reading indicates that you are treating the illness correctly. Do not try to suck it up and move on with life because that will not help you. If your body indicates you need rest, go take a rest. If you are unwell, seek treatment immediately and listen to what the doctor says.

Spirituality

This card signifies that you are not paying attention to your intuition. You are focusing more on the material part of your life. Do not let your logic overshadow your sensitive side. Spend time to focus on your spirituality. If you are working hard on your spirituality, this card's appearance in your reading can indicate you need to work on protecting and grounding yourself.

Reversed Position

Key Meanings

Controlling, obsessive, abuse of power, lack of discipline, father issues, lack of control, stubbornness, absentee father, rigidity

General Interpretation

If the card in the reversed position appears in your reading, it signifies that someone in your life with authority and power is abusing their position. This leaves you feeling rebellious or powerless. Having said that, the person is trying to give you the right advice and guide you, but their words are lost because of their behavior. The easiest way to deal with this is to be patient and calm. Only listen to the advice that works best for you and ignore the rest.

Always stand up to the way the person is behaving with you, but always do it in the right way. Lashing out at them will not get you the results you need. This card also indicates that the person you looked upon as a father figure has abandoned or let you down. If the card represents no individual in your life, it can mean you are letting your thoughts and emotions guide you. You must try to balance your emotions and logic. The card in this position indicates that you need to have structure in life.

Romance

This card in the reversed position indicates there is an imbalance in your relationship. It is this imbalance causing unhappiness and conflict. The card can also indicate that one person in the relationship is possessive, overbearing, stubborn, and controlling. This behavior only leads to a feeling of being trapped. This card in the reversed position shows there is a lack of balance in the relationship, especially because of the controlling nature, so both you and your partner need to find a balance.

If you are single, this card can indicate that your paternity issues are causing a destructive pattern for choosing your partner. Find a way to resolve these issues, so you can attract the right people. Your destructive thought patterns only invite people who want to take advantage of you. The card also indicates that you fear commitment and rebel against every characteristic of the Emperor.

Profession

If the card appears in the reversed position, it shows you lack focus and consistency for working. You find that the rules at work bother you and you need to change your place of work soon. There may be a different job in the same industry or another that offers more freedom. You may not want to follow orders and want to be your boss. Consider these options. With your finances, this card indicates that you lack control and need to get help from a professional.

Health

The card indicates you are not giving yourself enough time to rest and recuperate. You have a hectic routine that only causes stress. This routine can cause poor sleeping patterns, headaches, and other physical symptoms. You should not push your body too far since that will only lead to injury. Rest enough. If you have been taking good care of yourself, the card can indicate that you need to set a routine to improve your health.

Spirituality

In terms of spirituality, the card indicates that you should explore a different path to search for your spirituality. You should explore different paths, but you must ensure you trust and focus on yourself, even if you do come in contact with spiritual advisors.

The Hierophant

Upright Position

Key meanings

Traditional values, knowledge sharing, conformity, commitment, traditional institutions, marriage, conventional beliefs, religion

General Interpretation

This card represents institutions and traditional values. The card can either represent a mentor or counselor willing to provide you with guidance and wisdom. Alternatively, it can represent a religious or spiritual advisor, such as a rabbi, imam, vicar, priest, monk, or preacher who will guide you regarding your spirituality. When this card appears in your reading, it can mean you are constantly in touch with people who are stubborn about their beliefs and thoughts. The various institutions this card can represent include tradition, convention, religion, economy, family, social, social welfare, educational, medical, political, etc. The appearance of the card signifies that you should conform to tradition or convention. You should not try to rock the boat, but you *should* participate in ceremonies or create new traditions for yourself.

Romance

If you are in a relationship, this card's appearance in your reading indicates commitment and marriage. You can expect the relationship to move towards new milestones. The card indicates that the relationship is balanced on the same goals and values. If you are looking to answer a question on commitment, your relationship will turn a new leaf if this card appears in your reading. If you are single, it indicates you will begin a relationship based on security, commitment, and love soon.

Profession

If the card appears in your reading, it means you should start working with a team. Always do what is expected of you and do not focus on any unconventional methods. This is the only way to guarantee success. The card signifies that you will find a mentor or teacher who will share his knowledge with you. This knowledge will help you in your career. You can also become a mentor or trainer for your team. When this card appears in your reading, it can mean it is time for you to study at an established university. This is an excellent time to invest in conventional investment plans to avoid any risk. Try to stick to the conventional method of managing your money. Speak to an expert if you need advice on how to manage your finances.

Health

If you have any health issues, this card indicates that you should try to use conventional medicine. This is the best route for you. It is also a good time to set up a health routine in your life, such as taking vitamin supplements or exercising regularly. This is one of the easiest ways to boost your immune system.

Spirituality

Since the card represents spirituality, the archetype is considered the link between the higher power and you. If this card appears in your reading, it indicates there will be a spiritual advisor entering your life to help you on your journey. While this card is often associated with traditional beliefs and practices, if you do not believe or follow any traditional religion, the appearance of the card in your reading means you need to build a ritual into your spiritual practice.

Reversed Position

Key Meaning

Unconventional lifestyle, non-conformity, challenging beliefs and traditions, reversed roles, unconventional relationships

General Interpretation

When this card appears in the reversed position in your reading, it means you should break convention soon. You may want to change the rigid rules, traditional structure, and social norms, so it benefits everybody. The people around you will not understand why you are challenging things, and they may be against it, but this will not stop you from doing what you think is right. You will think for yourself and get rid of any traditional practices and beliefs that do not help you.

The card in the reversed position indicates you want to choose an alternative lifestyle of the way of living. The card's appearance in your reading can also mean you are clinging to all the traditional ways because you are ashamed or guilty. This will only lead to your detriment. Only when you learn to live the way you want can you free yourself from oppression. This experience will help you develop positively. The card in the reversed position can also mean you will clash with people in authority.

Romance

When this card appears in your reading in the reversed position, it means you want to be in an unconventional relationship or are already in one. You probably do not want to get married and are breaking tradition. You may also be in a relationship where the roles are reversed, and the people around you may constantly wonder or question your relationship. Alternatively, the card can also indicate that you and your partner are not seeing eye-to-eye, which is causing insecurity and conflict between the two of you. You need to be open and understand what your partner has to say. It is important to understand that compromise does not mean you need to push yourself out of your comfort zone.

Profession

If this card appears in your reading, it means you work with people who are rigid with rules. They never budge and always want people to do things their way. If this individual is your boss, you will no longer like to work in the same organization since you will constantly be at war with this individual. If you work with a group of people, it can mean that the team may ask you to listen to what the majority has to say despite their decisions' going against your beliefs. You may also find a mentor or teacher who may teach you how to challenge things in life.

Health

If you have been ill for some time, the appearance of this card in your reading is a sign you should try holistic or alternative therapies. These courses will benefit you and heal you faster than traditional medication, so do not be too rigid and change things a little. Find those therapies that work best for you. You may need to think out of the box.

Spirituality

When this card appears in your reading in the reversed position, it means you should let go of those traditional beliefs, especially the ones you no longer benefit from. Also, find the path that best suits you. You never have to follow traditional beliefs to be spiritual.

The Lovers

Upright Position

Key Meanings

Soulmates, love, partnerships, major choices, sexual connections, relationships, kindred spirits, shared values, desire, perfect unions

General Interpretation

This card signifies harmony, attraction, a perfect union, and love. If this card appears in your reading, it signifies that you are finding the balance in yourself. You have finally understood what you want and need. You also have a clear idea about your morals and beliefs and know what you value. This is one of the best ways to bring peace and balance to life.

When this card appears in your reading, it indicates that you will make a major decision. You are probably uncertain about people and situations in life, but the appearance of this card indicates that you will succeed in life. You will soon know what direction you need to take in life. Since these are important decisions, avoid taking the easy road. You must ensure you have the required information and choose the right path. This may seem difficult, but it is the only way to achieve great things in life.

Romance

If you are looking for love or relationship advice, this is the best card in the deck. This card is a soulmate card, and it talks about the bond that people share. If you are in a relationship, this card is a sign you and your partner will rekindle the relationship. The bond between the two of you will deepen, and you will learn to be more open to everything in your relationship. If you are single, this card indicates that you will find love soon. This relationship will not be infatuation alone, but you will love and respect each other. There will also be a deep and mutual understanding between the two of you. This card represents everything good about a relationship.

Profession

When this card appears in the upright position, it means you and your partner can start your company. If you have always wanted to start a company, this is the right time. You and your business partner are on the same page and can work together to set up the company. The two of you can support each other fully.

If this card arises in your reading, it indicates that you may find yourself romantically involved with a teammate or colleague. However, you should understand the risks and issues involved with mixing pleasure and business. This card also signifies that you need to decide about your career path. The decisions you need to make may seem undesirable, but this may not be the case. Gather all your facts and make the right decisions – a change in your role, a job change, etc. You should welcome these changes.

Health

If you have health issues, then this card indicates that you have the right support to overcome those issues. This support can either be a friend or partner supporting you. It can also indicate a healthcare provider or doctor treating you. This card can indicate that you have made the right decisions that will improve your health quickly. The card also relates to your heart health, so you must ensure you take good care of your health and heart when you find this card in your reading.

Spirituality

When this card appears in the upright position, it means you are working on finding a balance between your thoughts, actions, and emotions. This can only happen when you understand yourself better. This shows you your personal morals and beliefs, which leads to a stronger connection between your physical and spiritual self. This card in the upright position indicates you need to find a partner, so you can begin your spiritual journey together. You can take a meditation or yoga class together.

Reversed Position

Key Meanings

Trust issues, conflict, disharmony, lack of accountability, detachment, disconnection, imbalance, disunion

General Interpretation

This card indicates that you may be struggling to own up to your decisions. This only leads to conflict and uncertainty. You will never know where your life is headed. Remember that you can control your destiny. Never blame the higher power or energy, especially if you are the cause of your problems. Learn to be accountable for your mistakes and learn from your past mistakes. Learn to let things go. You also need to find a way to move ahead in the right way. Understand yourself better. Identify your beliefs and values, so you do not repeat the same mistakes.

Romance

If this card appears in the reversed position and you are in a relationship, it means the intimacy is great between you and your partner, but it means that the two of you are not on the same page when it comes to other important areas of your relationship. You both do not trust each other completely, and this makes it hard for the two of you to jump into the relationship fully. You probably have different values, hopes, and goals for the future, which makes it difficult for the two of you to connect. If you are unsure of the reason, consider the supporting cards to confirm the cause of the problem. Regardless of the reason, you both need to work on sorting the difference to ensure the survival of the relationship. If you are single, it means you will find the person you want to be in a relationship with, but this may not happen as soon as you had hoped. This card also means you probably choose the wrong people as your partners because you are unsure why you want to be with someone. This card indicates that you need to find a way to connect with a person before you jump into a relationship.

Profession

This card indicates there is disharmony between you and your partners. If you cannot communicate with your business partner, sit down with them and decide what you want to do with the business. Find the path your business will take. Find a balance with your partner so your business does not take a hit. This card indicates that you may find love at work, but you need to be cautious about it since this can only lead to trouble. It is important for you to understand the consequences of mixing your professional and personal life. When this card appears, it indicates that you will make impulsive decisions, and this can only lead to instant gratification, but learn to be accountable and avoid making the same mistakes repeatedly.

Health

With health, this card indicates you should learn to connect with your body and strike a balance between your health and harmony. You may feel that your body is not working for you but against you, but you need to learn to be kind to yourself. You also need to work with the current energy levels. Your body can do a lot for you, but sometimes, it needs rest. Never let your frustration get the better of you. Just give it time to heal.

Spirituality

With the spiritual aspect, this card in the reversed position indicates that you are only focusing on materialistic aspects of life. You want to fulfill all your dreams. This behavior will help you feel better, but this is only a temporary situation. It never helps you find peace and harmony. Always focus on the spiritual side and learn more about the true you. This is a better way to reward yourself. When this card is reversed, it indicates that you are sexually attracted to one of your spiritual advisors. If this advisor is seeking a relationship with you, then it means they are only doing this to abuse their power. This individual should guide your every move and help you on your journey. So, if they approach you differently, then you should be cautious.

The Chariot

Upright Position

Key Meanings

Hard work, focus, ambition, success, willpower, victory, determination, overcoming obstacles, self-discipline and control

General Interpretation

This card indicates that you can overcome various obstacles in life through focus, willpower, and determination. When this card appears in your reading, it indicates that you will feel in control, ambitious, and motivated. It is finally time for you to do everything you wanted to, but this card does not come without its challenges. You may face obstacles on the way, but you can overcome them if you stay focused. The card can also indicate that you may travel soon. It may feel like you are constantly at the battle, but do not worry since success is right around the corner.

Romance

When this card appears during a love reading, it indicates that you should work on conquering your emotions. This must be done if you want the relationship to succeed. If you have been going through a rough patch in your relationship, this card's appearance indicates you need to work with your partner to overcome your issues. If you are single, this card indicates that you need to let go of your past relationships, especially to move ahead in life.

Profession

When this card appears in your reading, it indicates that you are motivated and ambitious. If you have trouble with your colleagues, this card indicates that you need to stop worrying about people trying to sabotage you and focus on your work. If you are looking for a job, you may soon get the job you want. In terms of finances, this card is a good omen since it represents overcoming obstacles. Now is a good time to target any investments and purchases.

Health

If you have had health issues in the past, you will find the motivation to tackle those issues. You may take time to recover fully, but your willpower and energy will help to overcome these challenges.

Spirituality

In terms of spirituality, this card represents the start of a spiritual journey. You will have your fair share of obstacles and hurdles, but you can achieve success. Stay focused and be strong enough to try new things.

Reversed Position

Key Meanings

Being blocked by obstacles, lack of self-control, coercion, aggression, powerlessness, and forcefulness

General Interpretation

When the card appears in the reversed position, it indicates that you lack direction and feel powerless, so you need to control your destiny and never let outside forces change your course of action. Learn to control your life and do not go with the flow. You may lack confidence and feel powerless, which could lead to frustration and anger. Be determined to understand what course of action you need to take and the boundaries you want to set.

Romance

According to this card, you need to slow down. If you are in a relationship not progressing the way you would like it to, you must be patient. Trust that your relationships will progress the way they need to. Do not force things. If you feel like your relationship will move to the next stage, let it run its course. Do not be coerced into doing things you do not want. If you are single, the card indicates you will meet someone soon. While you should cherish the joy the relationship brings, do not rush into it.

Profession

You will still be motivated, but it indicates that you are not pacing your path when the card is in the reversed position. Take one step at a time. Let things run their course, and stop forcing your approach since this will be detrimental only to you.

Health

This card in the reversed position signifies that you will have a burst of energy and motivation. Do not rush into anything but take things slowly. If you are starting an exercise program, remember to take it slow. Do not do too much because you may end up hurting yourself.

Spirituality

The chariot indicates that you are ready to take on your spiritual journey. You must be mindful to never focus too hard on meeting all your goals. Let your spiritual path guide you and accept the rewards written in your name.

The Strength

Upright Position

Key Meanings

Overcoming self-doubt, control, taming, confidence, bravery, courage, inner strength, and compassion

General Interpretation

This card is associated with inner strength. When this card appears in your reading, it indicates that you can overcome any situation in life by mastering your emotions and thoughts. This card represents the strength you have to overcome challenges, similar to the Chariot, but his card only represents inner strength. This card indicates that you are strong enough to overcome any troubles and fears you may have. Since you are skilled, you can achieve success easily.

Romance

This card represents the constellation Leo. This means you can expect to have a relationship with a Leo if this card does come up in your reading. If you are single, this card indicates that you will meet someone soon. This is exciting news, but you need to see if the person is too wild for you. If you are in a relationship, this card indicates that you are a strong couple.

Profession

In terms of career, this card indicates that you should now work on mastering your fears, emotions, and thoughts, so you can forge ahead. You have the potential and all the skills you need to achieve this. Never let the fear of failure hold you back. To be promoted, then do everything you can so nobody overlooks you. With finances, you must make sure that you do not spend too much. The objective is to avoid making impulsive decisions.

Health

When you need a question on your health answered, this is a great card to get. This card indicates that your health is improving or that you are fit. If you have been ill, this card indicates that you will get your strength back soon. This card's appearance in your reading indicates that it is time for you to improve your lifestyle.

Spirituality

In terms of spirituality, this card indicates that you will connect with your spiritual self soon. This connection will help you find your inner balance and drive you forward to help you achieve your dreams. If you have had a few difficult days, this card indicates that you have the strength to overcome any obstacle.

Reversed Position

Key meanings

Feeling inadequate, low self-esteem, self-doubt, lack of confidence, vulnerability, and weakness.

General Interpretation

When this card appears in the reversed position, it indicates that you are not using the right strength to overcome obstacles. This card does not indicate that you are letting your fear control you. It is time for you to trust your inner strength to help you get out of a rut. You must find the strength to get out of your current situation. Always focus on the positive.

Romance

This card in the reversed position indicates that you are unresolved. You have self-esteem issues and cannot control your thoughts and impulses. This will always make you choose the wrong things in life. This becomes a vicious circle since a bad relationship will only scar you. Never let your fear or anxiety cause any problems in a relationship where there are no issues.

Profession

This card in the reversed position almost means the same thing as the card in the upright position. The card indicates you need to trust yourself and move ahead in your career. In the reversed position, this card indicates that you have always let your fear control you. Trust you have the strength to overcome any issues. Focus on your goals and work towards your end goal. When you are confident, people will be drawn to you, and they will notice the change. You may have an abundance of wealth at the moment, but this will not last if you are not smart.

Health

In terms of health, this card indicates that you are in good health, but you may lack self-control that can harm your body. Overcome these bad habits. Make small changes.

Spirituality

When this card appears in the reversed position, it indicates that you are connected to your spirit. Your emotions and fears stop you from connecting with your spirit. You need to find a way to let go of these fears.

The Hermit

Upright Position

Key Meanings

Solitude, soul searching, introspection, inner guidance, self-reflection, and contemplation

General Interpretation

This card in the upright position indicates that you have entered the period where you will attain spiritual enlightenment. You will find time to understand yourself better and remove yourself from your routine to understand your spiritual self. This card can also indicate that you want to isolate or withdraw to recover from hardships. This card indicates that you need to focus on yourself and your needs before focusing on helping others.

Romance

If you are single, this card indicates that you will find someone soon. You are coming out of the period of solitude and loneliness. You have had enough time to recuperate from a previous heartbreak. If you are in a relationship, this card indicates that you need to try to spend time with your partner.

Profession

This card indicates that you are focusing on making money and your career. You are looking only at materialistic pursuits and ignore activities that leave you happy. This card also indicates that you may wonder if you have chosen the right career. With your finances, it is time for you to be mature and invest carefully.

Health

This card indicates that you are overdoing things that can lead to injury. Take time out to breathe. Relax and rejuvenate your health. Take a minute every day to calm yourself and connect with your body. This is the best way to improve your health.

Spirituality

This card indicates that you should work on your spirituality now. You can choose any activity to help you connect with your spirit. Isolate yourself to do this. Focus on your spiritual side and give yourself time to listen to your inner spirit.

Reversed Position

Key Meanings

Paralyzed by fear, isolation, withdrawal, loneliness, being reclusive, restrictive, paranoia, and anti-social

General Interpretation

This card, in the reverse position, indicates that you have become reclusive. You may have had to remain alone for a short period, but you need to come back to the world and meet the people in your life. You can take time for soul-searching if you need to, but you also need to do it in moderation. You need to learn to draw the line at some point and determine if what you are doing is what you need to do.

Romance

This card in the reverse position indicates that you are lonely. If you are single, it suggests that you do not want to be in a relationship since you feel like you have missed your window. If you are in a relationship, it indicates that you feel like your partner is shutting you out. This card, in the reverse position, can indicate that you and your partner need to talk and communicate with each other.

Profession

In terms of career, this card indicates that you need to put yourself out there, network, and work on restoring business connections. You cannot work in solitude forever. It is best to work with teams and interact with the right people. This card suggests that you should make the right investment choices now with your finances.

Health

This card in the reversed position indicates that you may have mental health issues. The card is also a warning you need to give yourself time to relax.

Spirituality

When this card appears in the reverse position, it indicates that you spend time alone. You need to develop an interest in various activities so you develop spiritually. It is great to work alone when it comes to spiritual work, but it is also a good idea to connect with others.

The Wheel of Fortune

Upright Position

Key Meanings

Chance, destiny, cycles of life, upheaval, and fate

General Interpretation

This card indicates there are big changes coming your way. These changes are good for you, but change can never be easy. This is true even in the case that the change leads you to your destiny. The card in the upright position indicates that the universe is helping you achieve your goals. The card also indicates that your life is constantly changing.

Romance

If you are single, this card indicates that the universe is using its power to bring you closer to the person you are meant to be with. This suggests that you will have great fortune when it comes to love. If you are in a relationship, this card indicates that you and your partner may be ready to take the next step. This card can also mean there are difficulties that will creep into your life.

Profession

In terms of your career, this card is a good omen. It means you can expect changes in your job. If you have wanted to change your career or start your business, now is a good time. The universe will do everything it can to help you meet your goals. If you are stable and happy, this card indicates there will be big changes coming your way. These changes can be challenging, but they will lead to bigger things. With your finances, this card indicates that you will be comfortable. If you have had money problems, this card's appearance in your reading will indicate that things will improve for you.

Health

With your health, this card indicates that your health will improve if you have had health issues. You may also need to change your lifestyle. If you have been pushing yourself too far physically, emotionally, and mentally, it is time to slow down now.

Spirituality

This card indicates that fate is on your side. Spend time every day working on your spirituality. Use different exercises to help you develop and grow. Trust the universe and accept the signs it sends your way. This is the only way you can ensure that your situation improves.

Reversed Position

Key Meanings

Setbacks, external forces, unwelcome change, disorder, back luck, disruption, and upheaval

General Interpretation

This card, in the reverse position, indicates there will be a change in your life. This change is possibly unwelcome and negative. This card indicates that you will have challenging times, and it is time for you to adjust to this change. This change may make it seem like you have no control over your life. But this is not the case. When this happens, you need to take control of your life and situation. Learn from your past. Things may seem tough now, but there is a bright future ahead of you.

Romance

If you are single, take this time to understand yourself better. You may need to learn from your past mistakes and ensure you find happiness. You choose what you want to learn from your life. If you are in a relationship, this card indicates that your relationship is stagnant. You will find that the sparkle has gone out of the relationship, and you need to work on improving your relationship.

Profession

With your career, this card indicates that your career has stagnated. It also suggests there is uncertainty in your career. This card, in the reverse position, shows there are unwelcome changes coming your way, so you need to assess all the decisions you want to make about your career and see if you are making the right decisions. Understand this situation is temporary. Learn from the past and carry the lessons with you. This card indicates that you have not been careful with your money and need to set up a safety net for yourself in terms of finances.

Health

In terms of health, this card in the reversed position indicates you find disruption and issues in other areas of your life, creating a problem elsewhere. Never let pessimism get in the way. Change is often stressful, but realize that change is constant. You can determine how you will let the situation affect you.

Spirituality

With your spirituality, this card indicates that you may feel overwhelmed. You may feel the universe is not working in your favor. This will test your faith but remember that the universe has a plan for you. The trouble will pass, and you will come out more connected to your spirit.

The Justice

Upright Position

Key Meanings

Life lessons, karmic justice, legal disputes, honesty, truth, justice, and integrity

General Interpretation

As the card's name suggests, this card is related to legal matters, cause and effect, and justice. This card shows you that every action you perform has its own consequences, so you need to look at the situation and see what actions you have performed to bring you there. This card is also related to balance. This card signifies that your circumstances may change soon. Things may be out of your control, but it is your doing. Do not let the situation overwhelm you.

Romance

If you are single, this card indicates that you may find yourself in a relationship with a person working in the legal industry. This card corresponds to the Libra constellation. This means you may find a Libra in your life soon. If you have had trouble in your past relationships, this card indicates that your troubles will soon be over. You will emerge happier in the current relationship. If you are already in a relationship, the effect of this card's energy depends on how you and your partner behave.

Profession

If this card appears in a career reading, it suggests that you should pay attention to your life. You need to balance your personal life and work. Always take time out for yourself. True work and money are important, but not at the cost of letting go of some of your dreams. Make time for the people important to you.

Health

If you have had health issues in the past, this card indicates that you may be out of balance. It also suggests that you need to stop overindulging in some areas of your life.

Spirituality

In terms of your spirituality, this card indicates that you should focus on karma. This does not mean you will be punished for past mistakes. It only means you need to learn certain lessons in life, and the universe is helping you learn them.

Reversed Position

Key Meanings

Karmic avoidance, karmic retribution, injustice, unfairness, dishonesty

General Interpretation

When this card appears in the reverse position, it indicates injustice. This injustice can take different forms. It could mean you are being treated unfairly at work, and this affects you. It could also mean that people are treating you differently for no fault of your own. There may be a case where you were caught in a lie. So, do not let this happen. Ensure that you are honest if you are ever caught in a lie. Dishonesty only makes the situation worse.

Love and Relationship

If you are single, this card indicates that you are ready for a relationship, especially one you deserve. However, you have not learned from your past relationships, which makes it difficult for you to move on. You also make the same mistakes in your relationship because you have not learned. You may get caught up in the beauty of new love, but this does not help you. Take the relationship slowly.

If you are in a relationship, this position indicates that you are cheating or lying to your partner and will soon be caught. You can expect grave consequences. Any argument between you and your partner also may seem endless.

Profession

In terms of your career, this card indicates that you are not being treated fairly by the people around you. People may blame you for their mistakes, and there are times you may want to react but don't. You need to hold back and find the right way to deal with these people. This card, in the reverse position, also indicates that you have not been acting with integrity. Your behavior will cause problems. Do not avoid these consequences but learn from your mistakes. This is the only way you earn your respect.

Health

This card indicates that you need to find a balance between your personal and professional lives in terms of health. Spend some time everyday rejuvenating.

Spirituality

This card, in the reverse position, indicates that the universe is sending you learnings. You may be avoiding these learnings since you fear what may happen to you. You cannot refuse to learn these lessons since the universe will ensure you learn them in a bigger way.

Chapter Six: Cards 12 – 21

The Hanged Man

Upright Position

Key Meanings

Letting go, self-limiting, lack of direction, feeling trapped, needing release, confined.

General Interpretation

This card, in the upright position, indicates that you are in an unhappy situation. You feel like you are stuck in a rut or trapped. However, you fail to realize that you have the power to bring yourself out of this situation. You need only to change the way you look at the situation, and this will help you overcome all obstacles. This card also signifies that you are unsure of what direction you should take. It is important to remember that you cannot control every aspect of your life, and you need to let things take their course.

Romance

When this card appears in your reading, it suggests that you are not happy in your current relationship. It indicates that you need to step back and reevaluate your relationship. This helps you determine where your relationship is heading. This card suggests that you should make no decisions about your relationship now but need to think about the situation. If you are truly unhappy, you can let the relationship go. If you are single, the card suggests that you should let people; situations, or ideas go if they make you unhappy.

Profession

This card indicates that you should not feel uncertain about your job or career. If it has become stagnant, identify the steps you need to take to move ahead in your profession. Relax and let things take their course. If you rush, you will make the wrong decision. Your anxiety makes you feel like you have nothing when you actually do have enough to survive regarding finances.

Health

If you have been experiencing some health issues, this card suggests that you should consider every treatment option available to you. Do not reject the treatment you are undertaking but rethink the way you are tackling the problem. This card also indicates that the issue you are experiencing will take time to heal. So, do not get frustrated.

Spirituality

With the spiritual context, this card tells you that you should be careful about how you think of yourself. Stop engaging in negative thoughts and emotions since they affect the way you feel about life. You need to think positively and let go of thoughts and beliefs that do not work for you. This is the only way a whole new world opens up for you.

Reversed Position

Key Meanings

Stagnation, apathy, negative patterns, detachment

General Interpretation

This card, in the reverse position, indicates that you are only making wrong decisions. You are doing this because you want to distract yourself or change the way your life is. This card indicates that you are jumping from one situation and another without looking at how your actions are affecting you. Your attitude towards yourself and life will determine how you lead your life.

Romance

If you are in a relationship, this card indicates that you and your partner are holding back from each other. The two of you are only stuck to each other because you do not want to start over. The card also indicates that you can salvage the relationship, but you cannot confront these issues. If you are single, it indicates that you are sticking to the negative patterns only. You have not learned from your mistakes. Determine the pattern and try to work around it.

Profession

This card indicates that your career is not going in the direction you want it to when it comes to work. The card also suggests that you do not want to deal with the uncertainties. You may resort to blame the people around you and feel like you cannot change the current situation for yourself. This is the best time to control your life. Determine what you want to do and choose to do it. You may also need to gain a fresh perspective if needed.

Health

If you are suffering from ill health, this card, in the reverse position, indicates that you should find a way to resolve these issues. You can consider various possibilities and issues in life that are deteriorating your health. For instance, your grief and stress can manifest themselves in different ways in your body. It is best to use holistic or alternative therapies to improve your health.

Spirituality

With your spirituality, the card in the reversed position indicates you no longer know where you are headed. You have become shallow and do not connect to your higher self. This is a good time for you to explore paths to help you manage your situation. This is a good time to engage on a path that will bring you out of a slump. You will connect with your consciousness faster.

The Death

Upright Position

Key Meanings

New beginning, endings, transition, an unexpected upheaval

General Interpretation

This is a card that most people fear because of its name. It, however, does not indicate physical death. When you read tarot, refrain from predicting deaths. This is an irresponsible and unethical act. This card signifies transformation or change. The change may be difficult to undergo, and you may not accept it with an open mind initially. In the end, you will be happy about the change.

Romance

If you are single, this card indicates that you will get rid of your old issues, behavior, and beliefs since they are not useful for you. It is only when you embrace this change you can move ahead in your love life. If you are in a relationship, this card indicates that you are in a relationship you need to let go of. The relationship is no longer working for the two of you, and you are only clinging to old patterns. When this card appears in your reading, it indicates that it is time for you to let go of your relationship.

Profession

With your career, this card can be interpreted as a warning you should not depend on things that are not working for you. Change is always constant. If you are not happy with your job, then it is time for you to look for a new role. Start your business if you want to. When it comes to your finances, you need to be careful about your spending.

Health

As mentioned earlier, do not panic if you see this card in your reading. This card only signifies there will be a change in your health. You know how to handle this change because of your previous experiences. If you had ill health, you might be feeling pessimistic. You should, however, look for something positive and be ready when things change.

Spirituality

The death card represents transformation regarding your spirituality. In a spiritual reading, this card indicates that you can now connect with your spirit. You must learn to embrace this change.

Reversed Position

Key Meanings

Dependency, fear of beginnings, resisting change

General Interpretation

The Death card, in the reverse position, indicates that you are not accepting the change that will help you move forward. You do nothing new in life if you stick to your old beliefs. When you learn to let go, new energy enters your life, and this will lead to a bright beginning. Ask yourself why you are resisting change. If you are afraid, find a way to let go of your fears.

Romance

If you are single, this card indicates that you need to let go of negativity in your life. This is the only way you can bring positivity to your life. Work on your self-esteem and self-confidence. This is the only way you will be happy in life. If you are in a relationship, this card indicates that you want no change in your relationship. You are only clinging to the relationship because you fear being alone. The card also suggests that you can work with your partner to rekindle the flame.

Profession

This card indicates that it is time for you to change your career. You may fear this change because you cannot let go of financial security. Think about what is good for you and work on meeting your goals and dreams. With your finances, work on controlling your spending.

Health

In terms of health, this card indicates that you do not want to improve your health. You do not want to be proactive about your treatments. You may have old fears creeping in but learn to trust your spirit.

Spirituality

This card in the reversed position also signifies transformation. You may be going through a difficult time in life. You, however, do not like change. Have some faith in your spiritual energy and trust you will heal.

The Temperance

Key Meanings

Tranquil, soulmates, inner calm

General Interpretation

This card suggests peace, balance, moderation, and patience. This card indicates you need to find your inner calm and identify the right perspective of things. You need to change the way you look at things and allow yourself to be free of other people's issues. You must identify what you need to do in life and determine your actions.

Romance

If you are single, this indicates you should learn to find a balance in your life. This is the only way the right people will enter your life. If you are in a relationship, you are in a beautiful relationship. If you have had problems in life, this card indicates that you both will resolve the issue.

Profession

In terms of your career, this card indicates that it is a great time for you to set the goals to achieve your dreams. Your dedication and hard work will help you meet your goals. In terms of finance, this card indicates that you have managed your finances well. Having said that, you need to be careful about how you balance your savings.

Health

In terms of health, this card indicates that you need to control any unhealthy habits so you maintain good health. This is a good time for you to do this. If you experience health issues, you must look at the areas where you are not working up to your potential.

Spirituality

In terms of your spirituality, this card tells you that you need to follow your inner guidance. This card suggests that you need to find the right balance between your spirit, mind, and body.

Reversed Position

Key Meanings

Hastiness, clashing, excess, recklessness

General Interpretation

This card in the reversed position indicates an overindulgence or imbalance. This card suggests that you have been behaving in a reckless manner. The card in the reversed position indicates you have lost touch with your inner self and are behaving recklessly. But you are not looking at the bigger picture. You need to step back and see how you behave.

Romance

If you are in a relationship, this card indicates that you may have clashes and conflicts with your partner. This could be because you shower your partner with love, but he does not. There is no harmony in the relationship. So, step back and think about what you need to do. Calm down and reflect on the situation. If you are single, this card indicates that you are very open to people you want to be in a relationship with. Be not hasty and only get together with someone once you know them properly.

Profession

In terms of career, this card indicates there is a conflict at work. You may be working too hard, but the people around you do not appreciate your efforts. Since this frustrates you, you lash out at your co-workers. You need to restore the balance so the situation does not escalate. Regarding your finances, ensure that you do not spend impulsively. Be aware that instant gratification does not keep you happy.

Health

This card indicates that your body is imbalanced, which is leading to various health issues. The card in the reversed position suggests that you are not mindful of what you put into your body. Therefore, you need to connect with your body to determine how you feel and identify the issues causing you discomfort.

Spirituality

In terms of spirituality, this card, in the reverse position, indicates that you have a spiritual imbalance. The card suggests there is an imbalance between soul, body, and mind.

The Devil

Upright Position

Key Meanings

Depression, assault, depression, secrecy

General Interpretation

This card signifies addiction or depression. It may also indicate that you feel restricted or trapped in your relationship. When this card appears in your reading, it indicates that you may feel like external forces restrict you. This will leave you feeling victimized and powerless. Remember that you control your own fate. Therefore, you should never give up. Do not give in to instant gratification since this will not help you.

Romance

If you are single, this card indicates that you will only have an unfulfilling relationship if you are to ever get into one. The relationship may be only sexual, and this does not benefit you or your health. If you are in a relationship, this card indicates that you are trapped in the relationship. You and your partner may be codependent, and this type of relationship is unhealthy for you. If so, you and your partner should step back and determine what needs to be done to change the relationship.

Profession

This card indicates that you are trapped working on projects you do not like in terms of the career. You control your life even if it does not feel this way to you now. Evaluate what you want to do with your career and make the right move. Regarding the money, this card indicates that you should do everything in your power to help you maintain a cushion for the future.

Health

In terms of health, this card indicates that you may have trouble because of your addictions. If you feel you suffer from mental health issues, meet with a professional to discuss the reasons. The card indicates that you need to treat these and not let them define you.

Spirituality

In terms of spirituality, this card indicates you have become materialistic. Work on bringing the focus on yourself and non-materialistic aspects of your life. Do not spend too much time with people who mean nothing to you. It is always important to let go of things. Do not be critical or negative about things in life. Try to find a way to heal any negative feelings you may have.

Reversed Position

Key Meanings

Overcoming addiction, revelation, reasserting control, detachment

General Interpretation

This card in the reversed position indicates that you know *how* you have been trapping yourself in the incorrect things in life. This card indicates that you need to control your life and change the way you think and feel about different situations. The card suggests that you are learning to derive a new perspective from looking at different areas of your life.

Romance

If you are single, this card indicates that you may desperately seek romance. You wanted to be with someone, so you chose to be with whoever was available, no matter how toxic they were for you. The card suggests that you will soon learn to overcome these emotions and learn to be with the right person. If you are in a relationship, you and your partner may feel like you are stuck. It can also indicate that you and your partner did not do something that would end the relationship.

Profession

This card indicates that you know *how* your behavior affects your circumstances in terms of your career. It also indicates that you are finally ready to do what needs to be done to prevent this from happening. You will learn to take the right steps and do what you can to be happy.

Health

The card is a good omen regarding your health since it indicates that you have let go of harmful habits and have started to care more about yourself.

Spirituality

This card indicates that your mindfulness has made it easy for you to prevent any dangerous situations. The card suggests that the universe has let you go since it wants you to learn important lessons without having to go through difficult situations. The card indicates that you are finally coming out of depression, sadness, and anxiety.

The Tower

Key Meanings

Destruction, divorce, disaster

General Interpretation

You should not be wary of the death card but of the tower card since this is the bearer of all bad news. This card indicates that your life will go through a change, and you may not know how to deal with this change. The card suggests that you accept the challenge and face it head-on. This is the only way you can ensure that you have some peace and harmony in life.

Romance

If you are single, you may face a revelation about why you are single. This may not be a nice experience, but it will help you change for the better. If you are in a relationship, this card indicates that you are going through a rough patch. If so, you need to ensure that you let go. If you hold onto a relationship that needs to end, you are only giving yourself more grief.

Profession

This card indicates that you may not be in a secure job. It also signifies loss or redundancy. If this card appears in your reading, it indicates that you may see a change in your profession that will lead to better security and pay.

Health

This card indicates that you may befall an accident, so be careful about your surroundings. This card also suggests that you may have trouble with mental health, and this is understandable since the card indicates that you may go through emotional turmoil. The Tower is only a warning but remember that everything that is to come will pass.

Spirituality

This card represents the removal of old morals and beliefs that do not help you. You may have to reevaluate your beliefs because of an experience you went through. Understand this change will only open you to a new spiritual path.

Reversed Position

Key Meanings

Avoiding loss, delaying the inevitable

General Interpretation

This card in the reversed position indicates that you have avoided a difficult situation. To avoid such situations in life, you need to learn from your experiences. Everybody goes through hardships and learn from them. Do not hold onto those experiences and become bitter. Learn to let go of them and be happy that you came out of it.

Romance

If you are in a relationship, this card indicates that your relationship is over. You are only scared to let go of your partner because of how painful it would be. Face facts and accept things for what they are. If you continue to hold onto a broken relationship, you will only make it difficult for you to be happy. If you are single, this card indicates that you have prevented a disastrous relationship. It also indicates that you do not want to deal with the trauma of previous relationships, and you run away from the idea of a relationship. If so, you need to move on and learn from past relationships.

Profession

In terms of your career, this card indicates that you are working hard despite the difficult circumstances you are in. You may be doing this only to avoid unemployment. If you believe this job is not the right one for you, you should not stick to it because that will only make you unhappy. It is best to be out of your comfort zone so you can do the things you always wanted to.

Health

This card indicates that you have ignored a serious illness under the pretext it will go away. You have to face the illness head-on and see what you can do best to recover.

Spirituality

This card indicates that your old beliefs and morals are false, but you are afraid to let them go. You feel you would not be the person who you are today if you do not have these beliefs. However, you need to accept some facts and let go of those beliefs and morals that no longer help you.

The Sun, Star, and Moon

These cards are the simplest cards to read in the Major Arcana.

The Star

This card is the seventeenth card in the tarot deck, and it indicates swiftness, action, and movement. Some people also term this card as the wish card since it always gives the reader hopeful news. It talks about how a situation can improve and when you will achieve your dreams. The imagery is very easy to interpret. This image radiates a sense of serenity and peace.

If you have trouble with health or find yourself in a stressful relationship, the star's appearance in your reading will indicate a positive change. You need to improve the situation and continue to do better. This card suggests that you need to balance every area of your life. For instance, learn to pay attention to your loved ones and care for your health. This card indicates that you have infinite possibilities in your life. It is an optimistic card that helps you renew trust and faith.

The star also denotes educational and artistic matters, but it also suggests that your creativity will help you in your future endeavors. You will see your health improving if you were suffering from an illness. The star gives you a clear insight into your spirituality. You will finally learn to dive deeper into your inner spirit to learn more about your beliefs and morals.

The Moon

This is the eighteenth card in the major arcana and is associated with ripeness, fullness, and readiness. This card is associated with the constellation Pisces. Each section of the imagery has a significance of its own:

1. **Clouds:** Signify your fears and uncertainties

2. **Water:** Indicates your nature and feelings

3. **Reflection of the Moon:** Indicates you need to set your fears aside and learn to follow your intuition

When this card appears in your reading, it indicates that you need to listen to the messages from your dreams. This is the only way you can determine what the next course of action should be. The card also indicates that you should not trust people blindly. Be open with people, but not if they can cause harm to you.

The changing light in the imagery indicates that you should always look at the true form. If you are confused about a situation, take some time to understand what you can do to overcome that situation.

The Sun

This is the nineteenth card and is associated with pinnacles and accomplishments. This card's imagery defines everything the card indicates – happiness, enjoyment, love, romance, good health, and more. This card also includes all the elements. When the card appears in your reading, it indicates that you are out of the rut. This card indicates that everything will improve in the days to come.

The Judgment

Upright Position

Key Meanings

Forgiveness, judgment, decisiveness

General Interpretation

This card indicates that people around you are judging you harshly. It also means you are judging people based on how they present themselves. You do not give them time to warm up to you. The card also suggests that you have reached a state of mental clarity that allows you to evaluate yourself.

Romance

If you are in a relationship, this card indicates that you and your partner are too judgmental. You need to stop throwing the blame at each other and yelling. This only damages your relationship. It is best for you and your partner to sit down and speak. Make open communication a key element of your relationship. If you are single, you need to ensure that you are not hasty with your decisions. Take your time to determine if the person you are attracted to is the right one for you.

Profession

Regarding your career, this card indicates that you are constantly being evaluated or assessed. You may be in line for a promotion but would not know it. Always be careful about how you represent yourself. You are being watched.

Health

In terms of health, this card indicates that you will overcome an illness and feel whole soon. You have forged through difficult times, and your experiences will help you on the road to recovery.

Spirituality

This card indicates that you have learned everything you need to from your experiences in terms of your spirituality. You have identified the lessons that the universe wants to teach you and can now make enlightened decisions.

Reverse Position

Key Meanings

Unfair, false accusations, unwillingness to learn

General Interpretation

This card in the reversed position suggests that you are holding yourself back because of self-doubt and fear. Take action now. If you dilly-dally, you will lose the opportunities available to you. You also should not let people determine what you need to do in life.

Romance

If you are single, this card indicates that your embarrassment makes it hard for you to approach the person in whom you are interested. Never let your fear hold you back. Approach the person and know what he or she feels about you. If you are in a relationship, the card indicates that you and your partner are not willing to discuss matters that determine the relationship's status. Stop ignoring things. You need to know where the relationship is going and see if you and your partner are on the same page.

Profession

When this card appears in the reversed position, it indicates that you are at the turning point in your life. Your actions will make or break you. Do not be indecisive and seize every opportunity available to you.

Health

In terms of health, this card indicates that you need to let go of any negativity, especially if you suffer from an illness. Do not blame someone for causing you pain. When you hold onto negativity, you cannot recover easily. Accept your situation and let go of your past.

Spirituality

This card indicates that you are either refusing or ignoring your karmic lessons. The universe wants you to learn something, and if you ignore your lesson, the next lesson will be very difficult. You must give yourself enough time to learn so you can move ahead.

The World

Upright Position

Key Meanings

Fulfillment, success, travel

General Interpretation

This card signifies that you have the world at your feet. The card also indicates that new opportunities are opening up for you. You will also travel and be welcomed with open arms in other countries. Since you have worked hard to reach this level, go out there and celebrate.

Romance

If you are in a relationship, this card signifies that you have reached where you wanted to be. Maybe you wanted to be married or have children. You and your partner need to find a balance and make sure you are both on the same page. If you are single, this card signifies that you have many options available to you. Ensure that you are open to possibilities.

Profession

This card signifies that you will achieve all your goals. If you have set up your business, you will have reached your point of success. Now, enjoy the fruit of success.

Health

If this card arises in your reading, it means you need to overcome your health issues. This card is a great sign you will recover.

Spirituality

When this card appears in your reading, it indicates that you have learned what the universe is teaching you. You know who you are, what your path is, and how you fit into this world. You are in tune with your inner spirit, and your spiritual planes are opening up for you.

Reversed Position

Key Meanings

Disappointment, lack of completion

General Interpretation

This card indicates that you have achieved your goals, but now things have stagnated since you have nothing more to work towards. This means you need to throw your energy into learning something new or working on a new goal. Otherwise, you will be disappointed and feel like you are stuck.

Romance

If you are single, you need to go out and meet people. Do not let the feeling of loneliness creep in. You also cannot expect a person to come and knock on your door. If you are in a relationship, this card indicates that your relationship has stagnated. You and your partner both need to work on improving the relationship.

Profession

This card indicates that you have met all your goals. This signifies that you are not meeting your potential. Ask yourself if anything is holding you back or what you fear. You are the master of your life. Do not worry about making mistakes because that is how you learn.

Health

When this card is in the reversed position, it indicates that you need to revisit your treatment methods if you are suffering from an illness. If you are using the same treatments repeatedly, know that they do not work. Do not take shortcuts and work on the right methods to help you resolve your health.

Spirituality

This card represents the connection between you and your spirit. The reverse position indicates this connection is stagnant, and you need to find the will to progress. If so, you may need to try a different process. You cannot use shortcuts to learn more about your spirituality. You need to follow a path and try to learn more about your spirituality.

Chapter Seven: The Minor Arcana

The Minor Arcana may not be as important as the Major Arcana, but the cards do have some significance. The cards in the Minor Arcana tell you about the driving force of your life. It will indicate to you why you behave the way you do. It tells you about the concerns you may face in the future. There are 56 cards in this Arcana divided into four suits, just like the regular playing cards – Wands, Cups, Swords, and Pentacles.

Wands

The Wands is the suit that depicts creativity. The cards in this suit are associated with these qualities – self-esteem, self-confidence, enthusiasm, and creativity. They indicate to you your creativity.

Cups

This suit depicts your spirituality and emotional stability. When you pull cards from this suit during your reading, your interpretations of those cards help you better understand your emotions and feelings. You learn to understand what the higher power is saying to you and learn more about your feelings towards your partner.

Swords

The Swords depict your intelligence and way of thought. The cards in this suit help you understand your beliefs and morals. They indicate certain characteristics that help you understand your true self better.

Pentacles

This suit depicts all your concerns and fears, which could either be material or practical. They tell you what you most love doing and also whether you enjoy spending time with family and friends. The suit also indicates your perspective towards life.

Chapter Eight: Wands of Fire

This suit of cards is related to daily events, and they are connected to fire. When you work with wand cards, imagine you are working with fire. This means the cards you pick are volatile, full of energy, and temperamental. This suit is an indicator of your willpower. It is the source of all the energy in your reading. If a card from this suit appears in your reading, it represents your creativity and intelligence.

Upright Position

The suit of wands in the upright position indicates that you are a source of passion, inspiration, drive, and courage. The cards from this suit propel most actions you perform. You may also want to change aspects of your life using the energy from this suit. If the card is in the upright position during your reading, it indicates that you are an action-oriented, passionate, open, and adventurous individual.

Reversed Position

When the cards from this suit appear in the reversed position during a reading, it signifies weaknesses. The cards' energy in this suit is both powerful and destructive, and you should be careful when you use this energy. Fires provide warmth and light, but they can burn things to dust. This suit of cards is temperamental, and it moves from one end of the spectrum to the other in seconds. If this card appears in the reversed position, it indicates you are volatile and reckless.

The Cards

There are 14 cards, and the first card is the Ace of Wands. As you progress through the cards, you see that the cards in this suit are similar to a deck of playing cards. This means you have all the numbered cards as well as the four Court cards – the Knight, Page, King, and Queen.

Ace of Wands

If this card appears in your reading, be aware of a fateful or pivotal act you may perform, which will lead to a chain of events that will help you achieve your goal. This card refers to a new beginning or birth and the commitment you need to complete a project. It also indicates the beginning of a new journey. When this card appears in your tarot reading in the upright position, it means you should not take a bold step. If this card appears in the reversed position, it means you are not observing the signals and signs the higher power is sending you.

Two of Wands

This card is the second step of your journey. This is when you need to work on defining the plan to follow to achieve your goals. The plan you develop may need you to step out of your comfort zone. You learn to be more realistic and think about the long-term. This card in the upright position indicates you are making or will make the right decisions about life, while the reversed position indicates that you have created a deadlock for yourself because you are working with energies that cross each other. You may feel like you have taken up more than you can actually achieve. Always pay attention to how you feel about every decision you make. Do not jump the gun before you know what you want to do.

Three of Wands

When this card appears in your reading, it symbolizes a balance between your emotions and the journey you are taking. You will begin to feel more optimistic about your tasks and undertakings. When this card arises in the upright position in your reading, it indicates that you are someone who is adventurous and will do whatever it takes to meet their goals. You will be patient and learn to trust the right people. When it arises in the reversed position, it means you need to be confident and open about your ideas and learn to think big.

Four of Wands

This card indicates you should work with your team. It means you need to come together and create the right future for yourself. When this card appears in your reading, it indicates that you have the energy to begin your company. You need to work with others with the same energy as you to start the company. This is the only way you can create something positive to help you with the future. The card's upright position indicates you will start a new project or maybe get married. This card represents foundations. In the reversed position, this card indicates that you have forgotten to celebrate yourself. Therefore, it is time for you to celebrate every achievement you make along the way.

Five of Wands

This card represents the various struggles that one would face during their journey. In the upright position, the card indicates you demonstrate personal excellence, while in the reversed position, it indicates you are putting the people around you down to demonstrate this excellence. When this card appears in your reading, regardless of the position, ask yourself the following – who benefits when you fight hard to meet your goals? It is important to never let your ego guide you. If you do, you will always celebrate your successes alone.

Six of Wands

This card represents both recognition and respect for all the work and effort you are putting in to achieve your goals. The imagery on the card has a general who has led the troops to victory. This card often represents the victory parade. Since it took the entire army to achieve victory, but it was the general whose clarity and heroism led to victory. If this card appears in your reading in the upright position, it means you are doing well in your journey and will achieve success soon. If it appears in the reversed position, it means you need to trust yourself more and accept the praise and accolades people shower on you gracefully.

Seven of Wands

This card represents the people who can achieve their goals through willpower. This individual is accomplished in every way. If this card appears in the reversed position, it means you are letting your smugness and ego cloud your achievements. Your successes do not make you God, which means you can still make mistakes. When this card comes in the upright position, it indicates that you need to learn to stand up for yourself. Never let the fame get to your head. This will only make it harder for you to achieve your goals.

Eight of Wands

When this card appears in your reading, either in the upright or reversed position, it means the situation is escalating quickly. The appearance of this card indicates you need to accept change since it is necessary. You need to find the energy to keep up with this change. Understand that you cannot control things that happen in your life. If this card appears in the upright position, it means you need to find the energy to complete everything you have started now. Get busy and let your energy help you meet your goals. If it appears in the reversed position, it means you are wasting precious time.

Nine of Wands

When this wand appears in your reading, it means you need to rest for a bit. Give yourself enough time to restore energy, mend physical and mental wounds, and appreciate and enjoy your victories. There may be other obstacles that can arise during the process, but take a step back and assess the situation. It may be hard to do this, but trust that the people around you could take care of themselves and the project. If you make yourself irreplaceable, it means you do all the work yourself. If this card appears in your reading, it means you are considered irreplaceable, and this needs to change. If someone wants to help you, let them do it.

Ten of Wands

When this card appears in your reading, it indicates that you cannot rest and need to find a way to make it to the end. Otherwise, you are only letting yourself be vulnerable. Regardless of how difficult things may have become, do everything in your power to achieve your goals. When this card appears in your reading, it means you have taken up too much work to meet your goals. This card also represents the effort you need to make to complete the tasks in the queue.

Page of Wands

This card indicates you have a unique personality. You are independent and a nonconformist. You require nobody else's approval or affirmation when you want to do something. This card represents individuals who are rebels, innovators, or inventors. The card signifies freedom, and it holds a powerful message – one that says you have incredible power. It indicates you need to use the energy to achieve your goals. When this card appears in your reading in the upright position, it indicates you have a passion within you that will help you achieve your goals. It also indicates that it is time for you to explore and see what area of work interests you the most.

Knight of Wands

This card indicates you are a feisty and excited character. It also indicates you are easily provoked and are always ready to attack people who question you. You are filled with passion and energy and often fear no consequences. When this card shows up in your reading, it means your actions and attitude are intense. You must control your excitement and direct your energy in the right direction. You need to be intense in some situations, so *learn to control it.*

Queen of Wands

When this card appears in your reading, it indicates that you are a doer and leader. You will oversee the entire situation and ensure the team works well together. When this card appears in the upright position, it indicates that you are charming and charismatic. It also means you have infectious energy, which makes you lovable. In the reversed position, this card indicates that you need to be confident about what you do, learn to use your skills to lead your team with grace, and put yourself out there.

King of Wands

This card is a representation of the hero in you. Every individual is a mix of both feminine and masculine characters. When this card appears in your reading, it means you are an entrepreneurial, charismatic, and ambitious leader. This card means you never like sitting idly. You hate being bored and want to keep yourself busy. The card also means you want to lead a team and hate the idea of following another leader. You want to be loved and recognized by the people around you. The card indicates that you have immense energy and loves showering attention on the people he loves. You cannot control your emotions when someone crosses you. When this card appears in the reversed position, it indicates that you are too proud of yourself. It means you need to encourage the people around you and help them achieve success.

Chapter Nine: Swords of Air

This suit of cards is associated with change, conflict, and power. This suit of cards is associated with air, and if you see a card from this suit in your reading, it means you are looking for a solution to various external and internal struggles. These cards also mean it is time for you to make solid decisions. Let us now look at the different cards that make up this suit.

Ace of Swords

This is like the other ones or aces of any suit of cards. It indicates new beginnings. Since swords are often associated with discord, issues, and conflict, if this card shows up in your reading in the upright position, it indicates you have won. You may have struggled through the years to achieve your goals, but you are finally there because your hard work and zeal have paid off. If the card appears in the reversed position, it indicates that you are pushing yourself too hard. This means you need to calm down and relax. Let things take their course. If you keep working towards it without caring for anything around you, you will hurt somebody. The reverse position also indicates there are some people around you who are holding you back. Sit down and identify the problem.

Two of Swords

When this card appears in your reading, it indicates that you have trouble letting people in. If you build a wall around you, you can avoid being hurt by others, but it also prevents you from enjoying the great things destined for you. You should, therefore, spend some time to understand why you have your defenses up. Are you willing to let people in? If the card appears in the reversed position, it indicates that you are overprotective, either about others or yourself. This leads to some damage to the relationship. You must learn to be more open and let people do as they please. Give people some time before you judge them. You must understand the difference between stifling or suffocating the people you love and protecting them.

Three of Swords

It is unfortunate if this card comes up in your reading since it represents pain, heartache, and discontent, which are related to your relationships. Do you feel there is a love triangle? Do you find yourself feeling conflicted if you should be with another person? When this card appears in the upright position, it indicates you need to evaluate your relationships and make hard decisions to improve them. If the card appears in the reversed position, it means you can restore the relationship to its former level. All you must do is communicate, listen, and use your words carefully. This can help you and your partner overcome any silly issues that may have cropped up between the two of you.

Four of Swords

If you are feeling burned out or worn out, you are probably taking up more than you can chew. This card indicates that you need to step back and relax. Physical and emotional exhaustion could take a toll on you. You cannot function effectively if you do not give yourself enough time to recuperate. This does not mean you need to take a week off from work and spend it at the beach.

The card only indicates that you need to spend enough time at home with family and friends to rejuvenate. You can also spend some time determining the things causing stress and finding a way to relieve yourself of it.

When this card appears in the reverse position, it indicates that you are someone who was plagued with fatigue and illness, but you are recovering from it. Having said that, your body can heal physically, but it takes some time for your brain to move on from the negativity and stress. This position also indicates that you need to get up and move. Move on from the ailments drowning you and focus on the future, not your past.

Five of Swords

When this card appears in your reading, it indicates that other people's actions hurt you. This means that you need to speak to the people around you who are causing you harm. It could also mean you are hurting somebody. Therefore, be strong enough to admit when you have hurt someone. The card can also indicate that people close to you may betray you. Therefore, ask yourself if you trust everybody around you. You must remember to ask the right questions to determine who can betray you. You must ensure that you ask these questions discreetly. When this card appears in the reverse position, it indicates that you are someone who cannot let go of any discussion or argument. This happens even if you have won that argument. You need to learn to let go, especially when people know your opinion. Once you have voiced your opinion, do not gloat or take pride in your actions. Move on.

The card also indicates that you may have some repressed resentment over a past or recent argument you had with a friend or family member. You may have had a heated discussion with them and still are upset with the outcome of the conversation. These repressed emotions will only damage you since you cannot develop harmonious relationships with the people around you.

Six of Swords

From what you have read so far, you know that swords symbolize turmoil and conflict, but they can have a positive result, as well. This is one such card since it indicates that your life will only improve now. You have braved through the storm, and things are now looking up for you. You are at that point in life where things are only going to get better for you. The card indicates you have grown up as a person and have learned to do better and effectively deal with your problems.

When this card appears in the reversed position, it indicates that your situation has not improved fully. It is on its way to getting better. The card is a sign you need to evaluate how you can improve your situation faster. Should you speak to someone? Is there some action you need to take such things to improve for you? When you have your answers, go out and get things done.

Seven of Swords

This card is an indicator you are being deceived. The card indicates there is someone in your circle not being honest with you. Ask yourself these questions if this card appears in your reading:

1. Can you trust everybody around you?

2. Do you know if someone is keeping secrets from you?

The person deceiving you does not have to only be a part of your personal life but can be from work. Determine if there is some colleague with whom you cannot connect. Ask yourself if the people at work comment about you behind closed doors. When this card appears in the reverse position, it indicates that you are often frustrated because you find you are left out. You tend to feel betrayed when the people around you do not let you in on their secrets. You need to understand that the people around you are not leaving you out of things because they do not want to tell you but are doing so because they did not think the matter was important.

Eight of Swords

Do you have trouble with meeting your deadlines and achieving your goals? This card indicates there is something holding you back from living up to your potential. You are worried about what people may say about you or worried about failure. If you do not want to try new things because you do not know how the situation will turn out, you need to stop doing that. This thought process will never get you anywhere. Be strong and take the risk. This card, in the reverse position, indicates you will move forward in life because you know how to deal with your insecurities and fears. And you no longer let your frustration show when people around you do not live up to your expectations. This is an asset, especially if you hold a leadership position.

Nine of Swords

This card is associated with depression, misery, anxiety, stress, and other mental illnesses in new age traditions. This card indicates that you are upset about things in life and have nobody around you to speak to about your pain. You need to pick up the phone and find someone who can help you overcome these issues. If you do not speak to someone, the illness and sadness will overwhelm you and ultimately consume you. It is easier to bear a burden if you share it with the people around you. When this card appears in the reversed position, it indicates that you need to communicate with the people around you. The card in the reversed position is a stronger indicator you need to meet with a professional to determine how you want to overcome your mental health issues. Find the right mental health professional to help you overcome your issues. This card is a sign you need to address your mental health issues on priority.

Ten of Swords

In most traditions, this card indicates that you are grieving. This can be due to a relationship ending, a loved one passing or anything important that has to end. This card is associated with sadness and heartache. In the reversed position, this card indicates that someone around you wants to cause you harm. This is when you need to look around you and determine if someone is trying to look for different means to harm you or make you suffer. Determine if someone gains from your suffering.

Page of Swords

This card is known as the messenger. When this card appears in your reading, it means you should look at your life and see what matters to you in life. Your excitement and enthusiasm will indicate to you this is the time to start anew. You can begin a new relationship or even your company. This card tells you that now is a good time to do this. If this card appears in the reversed position, it sends you the message you may not have good tidings in the days to come. You need to determine if there are people around you who behave in an impulsive, immature, and erratic way. If you know who these people are, you should avoid them at all costs. These people will bring you only down and make it harder for you to move forward. Maintain your distance from them since their habits and activities may draw you into their negative habits.

Knight of Swords

This card indicates you have someone who is determined, loyal, and has strong morals in your life. This person could be you or someone very close to you. This card signifies the individual and acts as a reminder you should always focus only on the truth. Do this even when you do not like what you see. When this card appears in the reverse position, it indicates that your excitement and enthusiasm can be detrimental to others. Do you think your excitement to do something new has made it difficult for your friends? Do you ignore them when you start something new? Did you stop thinking or caring for their needs? If you have done this as a mistake, then you should recognize what you have done and ask for forgiveness.

Queen of Swords

This card, like the other cards in this suit, can represent a concept or an individual. This is, however, dependent on the situation. In most readings, this card represents a stubborn and aloof woman who is respected and looked up to. Her attitude makes her less approachable. Other times, this card may represent the concept you are not letting people in because you believe you are better than the people around you. People may like you, but they may also fear you because you are not someone to whom they can speak. Learn to be open and respect people's views. When this card appears in the reverse position, it indicates that you are narrow-minded and judgmental. You do not want to listen to anything new or different because you are not willing to change the way you think. You like sticking to tradition. You are against change.

King of Swords

This card indicates that you are a person in a high position. You can claim your authority. This card also indicates that you are empowered and strong. The imagery on this card signifies fairness, honor, and truth. In some traditions, this card refers to a person in a position of authority. If this card appears in your reading, take a minute to think about how this card applies to you. When this card appears in the reverse position, it indicates that you are rigid and narrow-minded. The card also implies that you are very difficult to speak to, especially if someone wants to approach you with an idea different from yours. You may come across as judgmental or harsh because you cannot tolerate new concepts, ideas, or people.

Chapter Ten: Pentacles of Earth

This suit of cards is connected to the earth and is associated with various matters of wealth, security, and stability. Any card drawn from this is always drawn to the North. The cards in this suit relate to security, home, investments, wealth, money, job, and other matters that are associated with important aspects of life. These cards are similar to the Major Arcana cards and the suits we discussed above. There are different meanings to these cards if they are placed in the reverse position. This makes it important to understand how to interpret them.

This chapter will look at what each card indicates in their upright and reversed positions.

Ace of Pentacles

When this card appears in your reading, it indicates that abundance and prosperity are around the corner from you. Trust your intuition, and take the risk to make new beginnings. When this card is in the reversed position, it means you can expect a change in your finances. You may soon have trouble with your finances and have a feeling of emptiness. This card indicates you may hit rock bottom soon.

Two of Pentacles

When you draw this card in your reading, it indicates that you are playing around too much with your funds. You are probably borrowing from too many people and cannot repay them. The appearance of this card indicates that you will soon receive help. When this card appears in the reverse position, it means the situation is out of control. Therefore, you need to give yourself some space to change the way you act.

Three of Pentacles

This card indicates that you will soon receive rewards for all the work and tasks you have performed. You can expect an accolade or raise soon at work. When this card appears in the reverse position, it indicates that you will quarrel with your colleagues and family. This will only lead to frustration.

Four of Pentacles

This card indicates that you are stingy or thrifty. You are probably doing everything in your power to complete your tasks and work, but you are probably working too hard and being very careful about all the money you have earned. When the card is in the reverse position, it indicates that you are insecure and cautious about all your finances and never want to invest in risky investment options. You only behave this way because of your experiences. Do not, however, let this experience affect your judgment.

Five of Pentacles

This card indicates that you are on the verge of ruin or financial loss. This card may also indicate that you will have a loss when it comes to your spirituality. When this card appears in the reverse position, it indicates that you have already incurred a financial loss. This may leave you feeling helpless, and you can get past these feelings by working on improving things.

Six of Pentacles

When this card appears in your reading, it indicates that you love to give. You enjoy giving because you do it for the joy and not because it will help people around you to like or appreciate you. When the card is in the reverse position, it means there is a matter of security you need to concern yourself with. It also means you need to refrain from treating people unfairly.

Seven of Pentacles

When this card appears in your reading, it indicates that you enjoy working hard. The people around you recognize you for your efforts and appreciate your work ethic. When this card appears in the reverse position, it indicates that you should begin to save money. You need to do this to protect yourself from difficult situations. You should, however, not be stingy and reward yourself whenever you can.

Eight of Pentacles

This card indicates that you are finally doing what you love doing most. You also are extremely good at what you do. Since you know your talents, use them to your benefit. When this card appears in the reverse position, it indicates that you need to work on fine-tuning your skills. Work on your talents and turn them into an asset.

Nine of Pentacles

When this card appears in your reading, it indicates you are leading a good life and are secure. It also indicates that you are content with what you have. In the reversed position, this card indicates that you or someone around you uses ruthless and manipulation methods to get their way. This behavior only leads to trouble.

Ten of Pentacles

If you draw this card during your reading, it indicates that you will soon become wealthy. So, do not let any opportunities go by. In the reverse position, the card indicates disharmony in both your personal and professional life. You must learn to stop quarreling.

Page of Pentacles

When this card appears in your reading, it indicates that you will soon meet someone who loves life. This person will change the way you look at life. In the reverse position, this card indicates there is a lot of information or news coming your way about your job.

Knight of Pentacles

If you draw this card during your reading, it means you need to learn to share your fortune with the people around you. Learn to use your experiences to help the people around you succeed. The reversed position indicates that you always want to be the best at what you do. You do everything in your power to achieve your goals no matter what happens to the people around you. This means you will find yourself alone at the top.

Queen of Pentacles

If this card appears in your reading, it indicates that you are a productive and easy-going person. This card also indicates that you have an abundant life. In the reverse position, this card indicates that you try to overcompensate for feeling terrible by making more money.

King of Pentacles

When you draw the card during a reading, it indicates that you are a generous and kind individual. It also means you may need the help of a financial advisor. In the reversed position, the card indicates that you are very insecure about life and need someone to validate your every move.

Chapter Eleven: Cups of Water

This suit is related to the element of water and indicates feelings and emotions. The cards in this suit also indicate the relationships you share with the people in your life. If you pick many cups in your reading, it indicates that you are looking for some answers to your questions on family matters, love, and other relationships. Let us now look at each cup's meaning and how you can interpret them in the upright and reversed positions.

Ace of Cups

When this card appears in your reading, it indicates that you will have a new beginning. Since a cup is associated with abundance and relationships, this card indicates that you may fall in love soon. This love does not mean romantic love alone. It can imply new friendships and beginnings. This cup is associated with good fortune and spiritual insight and indicates that a miracle or blessing will soon occur. When the card appears in your reading in the reversed position, it indicates that you can expect sadness and disappointment soon. It may also indicate these feelings do not relate to you but relate to the people closest to you. The card can also indicate that you need to be wary of the feelings of the people around you. Think twice about what you want to say to them.

Two of Cups

When this card appears in your reading, it indicates that an existing relationship will develop soon. The card may also refer to an insignificant relationship in your life, indicating that you need to learn more about that person. Focus on your current relationships and find ways to enhance and strengthen them. In simple words, spend time with the people in your life and stop worrying about meeting new people. When this card appears in the reverse position, it indicates that you and your partner have had a disagreement. This is driving a wedge between the two of you, so you need to step back and reevaluate the situation. Try to be the bigger person and raise your peace flag.

Three of Cups

This card is often considered the party card. Since the imagery represents rejoicing and celebration, it can mean that a happy event is right around the corner. Do you know someone expecting their child or getting married? You can also think about your family and see how happy you are with the people around you. Ask yourself how you and your family connect. When the card appears in the reverse position, it indicates that disharmony and discord are around the corner. The people in your life are not malicious, but this situation arises only because of some conflicts you have. Leave your emotional baggage at home when you head out to meet your family. Your bad emotions and feelings cannot ruin your day.

Four of Cups

When this card appears in your reading, it indicates you need to understand if your relationship comes with conditions. It is important for you to discover what your partner expects from you in the relationship before you take it any further. Do you feel you are giving more than you get? Or vice versa? If yes, step back and evaluate your relationship. A relationship only functions if there is a balance between the individuals who are a part of the relationship.

Ensure that the right people are in your life, and you like them. When the card appears in the reverse position, it indicates that your relationship is not as great as it seems. It may also have run its course. Sometimes, you may outgrow your relationship and find you and the other person have nothing in common. It could also mean the two of you no longer see eye to eye about certain issues. This means it is time for you to ask yourself the hard questions and determine if you need to break free of the relationship.

Five of Cups

When this card appears in your reading, it indicates that you are going through a rough patch. Since this cup is concerned with relationships, it indicates that you need to make some emotional sacrifices in your relationship. The card also indicates that you need to compromise and strike a balance with your partner. Compromise is not a negative thing. You may have to compromise a little to keep interesting pieces of information. The card can also indicate that you may be disillusioned or indecisive in the days to come, and this could happen if you are torn between two lovers. When this card appears in the reverse position, it indicates that you need to make a sacrifice soon. This time, the sacrifice is not an emotional one, which means you need to give up someone or something. You may not have been as attached as you believed, which makes it easier to let go.

Six of Cups

This card relates to all your memories. If this card appears in your reading, it suggests that some incidents and events in the past are significant and impact your present. These events may also affect your future. These events could be connected to your childhood or could have happened many years ago. The card shows that your past directly influences your present. It also indicates that you can expect some blessing from an admirer or friend. When this cup appears in the reversed position, it indicates that you need to be concerned about your recent memories. It also means a person with some influence over you is no longer a part of your life. That individual, however, still influences your decisions. This can either be good or bad, depending on the person's intentions. The card in the reversed position also indicates that you cannot let go of your emotions and baggage.

Seven of Cups

When this card appears in your reading, it indicates that you have many opportunities coming your way. You must, however, ensure that every decision you make is based on the larger picture. Stop focusing on what can help you in the short term. Do not be impulsive because that will not be beneficial to you. Always consider the long-term effect of every decision you make. What appeals to you now does not necessarily have to appeal to you in the future. This card may also refer to an individual using you for selfish reasons. When the card appears in the reversed position, it indicates that you are unhappy or bored at the moment. Since this is only a phase, be determined to give yourself some time. If you see an opportunity coming your way, grab it at the earliest and work on it.

Eight of Cups

Did you look at the waning moon in the imagery of the card? This image indicates that the relationship you did not give your full attention to is now ending. You need to accept that things have changed and move on. The card indicates that you will be disappointed in different aspects of your life. It can also indicate that you are seeking and wandering aimlessly. If this card appears in the reversed position, it indicates positivity. The card suggests that you need to reinvent and reevaluate yourself. You must learn to get rid of your old baggage and welcome new blessings and joys into life. This is the best way for you to move away from everything that has been holding you back. You must, however, be careful. Do not lose sight of your spiritual path.

Nine of Cups

When this card appears in your reading, it indicates that you finally have your wish. This card indicates both material success and emotional abundance. If you look at the card's imagery, it is a man who is happy and surrounded by cups. One assumption you can make is this individual is happy and has everything he needs around him. The card suggests that you have everything you want and are where you want to be. When the cup appears in the reverse position, it indicates that you have become complacent and have taken your relationships for granted. This will only lead to issues. Since the card also indicates abundance, it indicates that you are overindulging in pleasures when it appears in the reversed position. You must remember to stop wallowing in things that are great now because anything can change.

Ten of Cups

In most traditions, this card indicates happiness for the long-term. If this card appears in your reading, it indicates that your long-term relationships are growing and flourishing. You are finally at peace and content. In other cases, it may refer to a new beginning at home. This beginning could be anything from moving into a new home to getting married. If you look at the card's imagery, you can see a family looking at their house. This card only represents happiness and joy. In the reverse position, this card indicates issues at home. These issues will often sort themselves out, but you must be patient and compromise occasionally. The card also indicates that someone you trust may betray you.

Page of Cups

This card is like the other pages. It is known as a messenger card and means that the people around you are trying to grab your attention and want you to shower them with love and affection. This card may also indicate that you need to connect with people who are young and passionate. This individual is willing to do anything for you. In the reverse position, this card indicates someone who is moody and constantly wants your attention. This individual will do everything in his power to get you to notice them. If this card appears in the reverse position in your reading, it indicates that you may face obstacles and deception soon. It also indicates that someone doing something for you has an ulterior motive.

Knight of Cups

A cup card talks about relationships. This card indicates that you know how to stand their ground and stick to their morals. You, however, do not pick a fight with anybody over your morals and values. If this card does not refer to a person, it can refer to a new interest or passion. When this card appears in the reverse position, it indicates that you need to focus on people who want you to give them attention so they know they are doing well in life. There are some people in your life who want to be a part of your life for selfish reasons. Therefore, you need to watch out for deception and fraud. Stop committing to anything when it comes to the people around you.

Queen of Cups

This card, like all other cup court cards, represents a concept or person. This depends on the situation. In most readings, this card indicates that you are a sensual, understanding, and captivating individual. People around you are drawn to your charm since you are secure, honest, and loyal. If you are a woman, this card indicates that you are a great mother. The card indicates that you are someone who is kind and has a vision. When the card appears in a reverse position, it indicates that you are someone who is insecure. Sometimes, this card indicates that you are surrounded by people who are perverse and malicious. They use your insecurities and vulnerabilities to gain something from you.

King of Cups

When you draw this card during a reading, it indicates that you are someone who is ongoing and social. You are creative, entertaining, and outgoing. You also are skilled in numerous disciplines but are a master of more than one discipline. This is the card that most musicians, spiritual seekers, and artists want. When this card is in the reverse position, it indicates that you are a person with insecurities due to previous relationships. You are probably prone to depression. This person also has the authority and will do everything in their power to step over someone without thinking twice. You, however, need to be careful about these characteristics. You also need to ensure you never let people take advantage of you.

Chapter Twelve: Tips to Deepen Your Understanding of Tarot Symbolism

There are a lot of books and articles published over the years on Tarot reading. When you look at Tarot cards for the first time, you will feel overwhelmed. You may be very confused about whom you need to listen to and what interpretation you need to give your seeker. The truth is there is often no right answer.

There is a picture on every tarot card. These cards tell a story. You can use the story to help you connect with your subconscious mind. This interpretation is personal to you, and thus the interpretation varies from one person to the other. This book gives you the meaning behind the cards. You, however, need to practice before you begin Tarot reading.

When you work with these cards, you tend to develop an affinity towards some cards. If you use the technique detailed in the first chapter, you will connect with any card placed in front of you. These flashes of intuition leave you with a meaning that may contradict your previous understanding of the card. It is for this reason you need to choose a deck you connect with. This helps you develop your interpretations of the cards.

Once you choose a deck you connect with, it becomes easier for you to interpret the meaning. You can use the booklet to help you understand the meaning. Before you do this, place the cards in front of you and pick one. You can start with the Fool. Look very closely at the card, the colors, and the symbols on it. Try to determine what the picture means to you. Ask yourself these questions:

Does the card remind you of a certain event in your life, or does it remind you of a person? Do you relate to the situation in the picture? It is great if you do. You could then pick up another card and examine it as you did to the first. Then place that card next to the first card. Can you connect the two cards to each other? Is there a story? Continue to look at the cards. You will learn to build a story to help you answer different questions. See how things have changed from one point in the story to another.

Try to act like you are telling the story to someone. Look at the cards and use the image to help you come up with the story. Let your intuition control you. It may feel like imagination, but you are doing the best you can with your cards. This is the best way to connect to your subconscious and your intuition or your client to help you learn to read the Tarot cards.

When you read the cards for another person, you need to describe to them what is happening in the pictures. You will find yourself giving them an accurate reading. This will only come with time and practice.

When you have learned to read tarot cards, you will interpret the cards in front of you easily. You will learn to use stories to read the cards. Remember there is always a story you can read.

Conclusion

If you are a beginner, this book can act as your guide. It covers the information you need to know about tarot. It tells you how to interpret the meanings of the cards in the deck. There are different spreads that are used across the world. The book covers three spreads that are used often, and if you are a beginner, it is safe to use these spreads. This book also works as a refresher if you are an experienced tarot reader.

You are bound to make mistakes as a beginner but do not let this bring you down. If you are unsure or hesitant to perform a reading, do one for yourself. Practice as often as you can. You can use the meanings and interpretations in this book to help you develop the right interpretation.

The book takes you through each card in the major and minor arcana. It details the different ways these cards can be interpreted. When you begin with tarot reading, use these interpretations to help you. You will soon learn to interpret with ease. I hope the information in the book helps you with reading the cards well.

Here's another book by Mari Silva that you might like

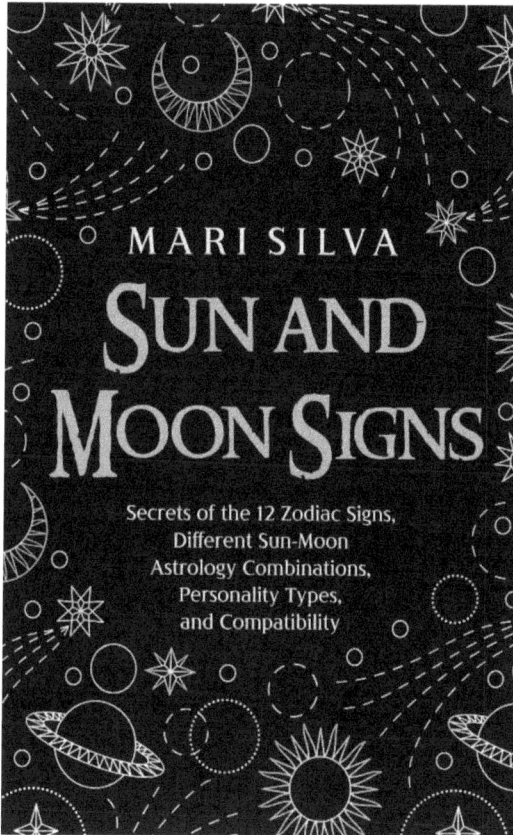

MARI SILVA

SUN AND MOON SIGNS

Secrets of the 12 Zodiac Signs,
Different Sun-Moon
Astrology Combinations,
Personality Types,
and Compatibility

References

Chariot Tarot Card Meanings. (n.d.). Biddy Tarot website: https://www.biddytarot.com/tarot-card-meanings/major-arcana/chariot/

Payne-Towler, C. (n.d.). Tarot Suits: The Swords Cards. Tarot.com website: https://www.tarot.com/tarot/cards/suit-of-swords-meaning

Payne-Towler, C. (n.d.). Tarot Suits: The Wands Tarot Card Meanings. Tarot.com website: https://www.tarot.com/tarot/cards/suit-of-wands-meaning

Ranie, B. (2010, July 8). Tarot Card Meanings - The Star, the Moon, and the Sun. https://ezinearticles.com/?Tarot-Card-Meanings---The-Star,-the-Moon,-and-the-Sun&id=4627219

Suit of Pentacles Tarot Card Meanings. (n.d.). Biddy Tarot website: https://www.biddytarot.com/tarot-card-meanings/minor-arcana/suit-of-pentacles/

Suit of Wands Tarot Card Meanings. (n.d.). Biddy Tarot website: https://www.biddytarot.com/tarot-card-meanings/minor-arcana/suit-of-wands/

The Major Arcana Tarot Card Meanings. (2020, September 23). Tarot.com website: https://www.tarot.com/tarot/cards/major-arcana

The Major Arcana. (n.d.). thetarotguide website: https://www.thetarotguide.com/major-arcana

The Suit of Pentacles Tarot Card Meanings. (2020, January 28). Labyrinthos website: https://labyrinthos.co/blogs/tarot-card-meanings-list/the-suit-of-pentacles-tarot-card-meanings

The Suit of Wands Tarot Card Meanings. (2020, January 28). Labyrinthos website: https://labyrinthos.co/blogs/tarot-card-meanings-list/the-suit-of-wands-tarot-card-meanings

Wigington, P. Learn Religions website: https://www.learnreligions.com

Aprile, C. (2017, November). It's All Connected! The Importance of Numerology in the Tarot. www.astrology.com website: https://www.astrology.com/article/its-all-connected-the-importance-of-numerology-in-the-tarot/

Bender, F. (2015, April 12). The Maturity Number. Felicia Bender website: https://feliciabender.com/the-maturity-number/

Bunn, M. (n.d.). Ayurveda & Vedic Science: The Science of Life. markbunn.com.au website: https://markbunn.com.au/blog/ayurveda-vedic-science-the-science-of-life

Felicia. (2017, March 23). What Your Destiny Number Reveals About Your Life Purpose. Felicia Bender website: https://feliciabender.com/the-destiny-or-expression-number/

Galbraith, A. (2019, December 19). How to find your personal year number. Where She Grows website: https://whereshegrows.com/how-to-find-your-personal-year-number/

Kuna, N. (n.d.). The 9-Year Cycle in Numerology. NATALIA KUNA: Psychic & Energy Healer. Founder of "Spiritual Course Academy" (coming soon). https://www.nataliakuna.com/ website: https://www.nataliakuna.com/the-9-year-cycle-in-numerology.html

Lad, V. (2019). Ayurveda: A Brief Introduction and Guide. Ayurveda.com website: https://www.ayurveda.com/resources/articles/ayurveda-a-brief-introduction-and-guide

Overview of Astronumerology. (n.d.). Astronumerology Wisdom website: https://www.astronumerologywisdom.com/overview-of-astronumerology.html

Numerology. (n.d.). The Meaning Of The Name website: https://themeaningofthename.com/numerology-calculator/

Numerology Of Your Birth Date – Your Destiny Decoded In Your Life Path. (n.d.). Kari Samuels website: https://karisamuels.com/life-path-number/

Numerology Calculator: Your Life Path Number And Meaning. (2015, December 15). The Law Of Attraction website: https://www.thelawofattraction.com/life-path-number-challenges/

Numerology: History, Origins, & More - Astrology.com. (2019). Astrology.com website: https://www.astrology.com/numerology

Numerology + Life Cycles. (n.d.). Flow and feels website: https://flowandfeels.com/blog/numerology-life-cycles

Samuels, K. (n.d.). Numerology Of Your Name – Your Destiny Decoded. Kari Samuels website: https://karisamuels.com/numerology-of-your-name/

The Connection Between Numerology And Astrology - Astroyogi.com. (n.d.). www.astroyogi.com website: https://www.astroyogi.com/articles/the-connection-between-numerology-and-astrology.aspx

Wilson, T. (2007, March 28). How Numerology Works. HowStuffWorks website: https://science.howstuffworks.com/science-vs-myth/extrasensory-perceptions/numerology.htm

www.ingramcontent.com/pod-product-compliance
Lightning Source LLC
Chambersburg PA
CBHW071856090426
42811CB00004B/636